HOW *Not* TO
WRITE

HOW Not TO WRITE

Simple Guidelines for the Grammatically Perplexed

Terence Denman

Copyright © 2005 by Terence Denman

First published in Great Britain in 2005 by
Piatkus Books Ltd
5 Windmill Street, London W1T 2JA
email: info@piatkus.co.uk

This edition published in 2007

The moral right of the author has been asserted

A catalogue record for this book is available from the British Library

ISBN 0 7499 2703 8

Text design by Briony Chappell

This book has been printed on paper manufactured with respect for the environment using wood from managed sustainable resources

Typeset by Palimpsest Book Production Limited, Grangemouth, Stirlingshire

Printed and bound in Great Britain by
Clays Ltd, St Ives plc

CONTENTS

INTRODUCTION

You may have surprised yourself by buying (or are you just 'browsing' and thinking of buying?) a grammar book. To do so you may have overcome a lifelong grammarphobia. Grammar has a reputation for being as interesting as watching paint dry. But this is not the usual grammar book. It even contains a few jokes. They're not very good jokes, it's true. But then, you haven't paid very much for this book, have you?

Indeed, this is not a traditional grammar book. I don't look at many parts of English grammar. I wouldn't want to stop you studying grammar in more detail, but this book concentrates on the grammar that will help office writers improve the power of their writing. The grammar they need is what will help them write clearly and concisely, and without making errors that will annoy their readers and give a bad impression of their organisations.

Business writing doesn't have to be particularly stylish. Office writing is often giving important information, but it's information that doesn't usually have a long shelf life. No one will take down your collected memos in a hundred years and read them for entertainment (unless they lead a sad life). So we're not aiming for the Nobel prize for literature. If you're working on a novel about the steamy goings-on in your office, I wish you well. I'll be the first one to buy a copy when it arrives in the bookshops (and I can't wait for the film). But that kind of writing is very different from what we are trying to do in day-to-day office and business writing.

That doesn't mean you shouldn't (or couldn't) write more effectively at work. Much office writing is mediocre, or worse. You sometimes have to read it several times to get the meaning. And it may say in many words what could have been said in few. Oddly, sloppiness and inefficiency that we wouldn't tolerate elsewhere in the office we put up with in writing.

The Four Cs

Why have you bought this book? The answer may surprise you: you bought the book because you are a professional writer. You probably spend most of your working day writing, worrying about the writing you do, or reading your colleagues' writing (which isn't always a pleasure). We all say on our CVs that we have 'excellent written communication skills'. But is that always true?

Writing is easily the most neglected skill at work. Staff attend courses in IT, team building, health and safety, and so on. All very useful. But writing, their main task, is neglected. Will you or your staff write naturally as angels? Probably not. And when you start writing in an office, especially if you're young and inexperienced, you tend to write in the same way as the people around you. You get drawn into the company style. All too often, that is not an effective style. Practice, far from making perfect, tends to ingrain bad habits.

Good business writing should aim for the **four Cs**.

Good business writing is **correct**. It gives the reader correct information, *and* uses correct grammar, spelling and punctuation. Poor grammar won't impress your readers, and it will make your writing more difficult to understand. I'm talking about real grammar, of course, and not some of the myths that I look at in this book (myths that will damage your writing rather than improve it).

Good business writing is **clear**. So clear that the reader has to read it only *once* to get the meaning. Remember that clarity, like beauty, is in the eye of the beholder. You can't be the best judge of how clear your writing is. You have to step outside your writing and look at it from the readers' point of view. How would they understand it without the prior knowledge that you bring to the subject? You may need to try out the leaflets, forms and procedures that you write on potential readers.

Good business writing is **concise**. There is too much waffle about. Many office writers don't 'red-pen' their writing before they send it out. Don't be rude or abrupt of course. But wasting your readers' time *is* rude. Who remembers the myth of the 'paperless office'? I never thought it would happen. There's more paper around than ever before. You can't move for it. So, while we all wait for the paperless office to arrive (in about AD 3050 at this rate), we should all be doing our best to make sure that we are not contributing unnecessarily to the ocean of paper that surrounds us. If you don't take the time to cut the waffle, then you waste the time of your colleagues and customers. I think it was Pascal who wrote to a friend saying, 'I'm sorry this is a long letter, I didn't have time to write you a short one.' Think about it.

Good business writing is **conversational**. Too much office writing gets into a tangle by moving too far away from the everyday words that we use when we're talking to someone. It's a good idea to *listen* to anything you have written. Then ask yourself whether you would have used the same words if you had been explaining it face to face or on the phone. I'm not quite saying 'write as you speak'. We swear when we speak (some of us!), we use slang, and we don't always speak in proper grammatical sentences. So don't end your sentences with 'innit'! But the everyday words are the ones to go for wherever possible. They're easier to understand, they're usually shorter and they give your writing a more natural and human tone.

Be warned, this book does expect you to do a few exercises. But don't think of this as going back to school. There's no better way of applying your new grammatical knowledge than by attempting to put it into practice. Making mistakes doesn't matter, so resist the temptation to look at my rewrites before you've had a go yourself. We all (well most of us) learn from our mistakes. 'Gain from pain', as I call it, should be exactly that – the gain will be permanent, the pain temporary.

I have also included at the back of the book a short A-to-Z glossary of the most important grammatical terms. From now on, all grammar terms in bold in the text will be in the glossary.

Throughout the book I've sprinkled a few choice examples of how not to write by quoting from some of the Plain English Campaign's annual 'gobbledygook awards' (Golden Bulls) winners, from some runners-up and from a few low points of writing that I've spotted on my own journey through life. They're all genuine, though you may find that difficult to believe. You didn't write any of them, did you? If you did, you will certainly find this book useful.

GRAMMAR TIP 1
Life and Death Sentences

Let me introduce you to the full stop. Clutch it to your bosom. You've got a friend. And, like any true friend, he (or she, because no one knows the sex of a full stop) will be there when you need him (or her). And you will. Because good writers use the full stop more than any other punctuation. For good writers know the power of the sentence.

Words are the basic building blocks of writing. But words don't make sense until we form them into sentences. We all think we know what a sentence is ('What comes between two full stops,' I hear you shout). In fact, no grammar book will ever give you a watertight definition of a sentence – because there isn't one. But, though they are difficult to define, we must get our sentences right if we want to write effectively.

From our practical point of view, the best way to define a sentence is to say that it contains an idea. But often a sentence contains too many ideas, because it is too long. And when sentences are too long there is also a worrying tendency for them to fall apart grammatically, as well as to overburden the poor reader with too much information at once.

The Long and Short of It

Faced with a long, and often badly written, sentence, most of us go back and read it again slowly, breaking it into ideas. And then we mentally put in the full stops that the writer was too lazy to supply. This is not acceptable. *Long sentences are death sentences.* They are *death* to any possibility of a clear and punchy writing style. Short sentences put *life* into your writing.

We divide sentences grammatically into three types. The **simple sentence** has one idea in it:

I like your new shoes.

The **compound sentence** has at least two ideas in it, which are independent and could have been two sentences. We generally use a joining word (a **conjunction**) such as *and*, *but* or *or* to link the ideas:

I like your new shoes, but I don't like your new suit.

The **complex sentence** has a main idea, and at least one subordinate idea that depends on the main idea.

The subordinate idea is often introduced by words such as *when, because, although, if, since, that*:

I revised the report when the new sales figures came in.

It wouldn't be sensible to break the compound sentence shown here in two. And we couldn't break the complex sentence into two unless we rewrote it. So I'm not suggesting that you use only simple sentences. Your writing would sound childish and staccato. Don't put in a full stop just because you could do so grammatically. Look for main ideas, but remember that the main idea may include one or two related ideas that it would be silly or dangerous to break into separate sentences.

> Office workers often feel that they are undervalued, and that they need more praise from management. But, when one worker received this comment from his boss, he was so puzzled that he sent it to the Plain English Campaign.
>
> `I admire your focused attention to screening the quantum of remaining potentiality vs. the generic strategic quantum of growth potentiality that we are now trying to seek access to.`
>
> I think this means 'must try harder'!

Aim for an average of 18 words a sentence. I emphasise *average*. Don't try to make all your sentences exactly 18 words long. That way madness lies. You will have many sentences shorter than 18 words. But look closely at any sentence with 25 words or more. We won't ban them, because that would be stupid. But probably you've got more than one main idea in a sentence that long.

Vary your sentence length occasionally, especially in a long document. Even short sentences can become monotonous and annoy the reader.

Salvaging Long Sentences

When you spot a long sentence, you may decide that it's such a mess that it would be better to junk it and start again. But many long sentences are salvageable if you adopt one or more of three suggestions.

First, look at any comma or semicolon in a long sentence. You can often (not always) change the comma to a full stop. The presence of several commas in a sentence almost certainly means that one of them would be doing better service for its country as a full stop. And remember that semicolons are more useful in literary rather than office writing. If you're using a semicolon correctly (and many writers don't), then you can always replace it with a full stop. Do so. A semicolon is a full stop with an identity problem.

Second, look for any 'connecting' words, such as *and*, *but*, *because*, *although*, *since*, *or*, *however* and so on. A connecting word in a short sentence can be left alone. But if you spot a connecting word in a long sentence, try putting a full stop before it. The connecting word may tell you that you are moving on to a new idea, making an idea that opposes the one you've just made, or reinforcing that idea with more information.

Third, see if you can turn the sentence into a bulleted list. Generally, this works best with a long sentence that contains three or more closely connected pieces of information.

Shortening sentences when you edit will bring three benefits. First, your reader will be able to take in your points quickly. Second, you will have more chance of getting your ideas in the right order. And, third, you will cut some of the waffle out of your writing. The last advantage is especially important. Long sentences hide redundant words. Once you shorten the sentences, the little swine come out of the undergrowth and you can shoot them down.

Waste Not

One common cause of long sentences is when writers waste words at the beginning of the sentence. Things such as 'It will be noted that …', 'I have to advise you that …', 'It is further suggested that …' Don't do this. It's the writing equivalent of athletes warming up before they get on the track, or clearing your throat before you start to speak. The worst sentence opener I have seen lately was 'And in addition I would add that …' I had to go for a long walk after reading that one. When you're editing, hover like a vulture over the first words of your sentences. If they shouldn't be there, then swoop in and remove them.

When you start putting your full stops in a long sentence, do make sure that what you've got either side of the full stop makes sense as a grammatical sentence. One popular 'rule' of grammar that isn't really a rule is that you must have at least one **verb** (the 'doing' word) in a sentence. Certainly, don't have too many verbless sentences, or you will end up writing in a very strange manner. Like this. Or this. Or perhaps this. But the occasional verbless sentence can be dramatic and effective. All right?

By the way, the grammar check on most computers spots only *very* long sentences (generally more than 50 words). You may need to get your machete out long before this.

One final point. Once you've got your sentences short, don't let your paragraphs become long. Aim for an average of five or six sentences to a paragraph. And the occasional single-sentence paragraph can help to emphasise an important point. There's nothing more intimidating to readers than great slabs of unbroken text. Make sure your paragraphs are always wider than they are deep.

Exercise: Gain from Pain

Now get that machete out and chop up some boa constrictors into grass snakes. Don't change meaning, but remember that you may have to do a little bit of rewriting to 'mend the breaks' as you shorten sentences.

1. Our current top-management structure is too complex and confusing, and leads to a loss of manufacturing efficiency because it takes a long time to make a decision and even longer to implement it at factory floor level, and this also means that we cannot respond to improvements in technology and design quick enough.

2. Only one-third of home mortgage loans were for first-time buyers in January to March of this year, however the proportion of lending to first-time buyers has been declining steadily for the last few years, probably reflecting increased affordability problems because of rising house prices, and the growth in the rental market.

3. Production difficulties will continue for some time according to the latest reports from our line managers, so we expect therefore that actual spending is likely to be higher than the budget allocations we set last April, but this will depend on levels of production between now and the end of the year.

4. I will need a draft copy of your report on the present computer system by 7 May, and then we could meet here on 12 May to discuss any problems about what new equipment to buy so that you could then prepare the final draft of the report for submission to the IT development working group in June.

5. Fears that oil reserves are nearly exhausted are nothing new, as more than eighty years ago, the head of the US Geological Survey predicted that American oil reserves would run out in a few years and he advised the US government to take steps to secure new supplies from the Persian Gulf.

Possible Rewrites

1. Our current top-management structure is too complex and confusing. This leads to a loss of manufacturing efficiency, because it takes a long time to make a decision and even longer to implement it at factory floor level. It also means that we cannot respond to improvements in technology and design quickly enough.

2. Only one-third of home mortgage loans were for first-time buyers in January to March of this year. However, the proportion of lending to first-time buyers has been

declining steadily for the last few years. This probably reflects increased affordability problems due to rising house prices and the growth in the rental market.

3. Production difficulties will continue for some time, according to the latest reports from our line managers. We expect, therefore, that actual spending is likely to be higher than the budget allocations we set last April. But this will depend on levels of production between now and the end of the year.

4. I will need a draft copy of your report on the present computer system by 7 May. We could meet here on 12 May to discuss any problems about what new equipment to buy. You could then prepare the final draft of the report for submission to the IT development working group in June.

5. Fears that oil reserves are nearly exhausted are nothing new. More than eighty years ago, the head of the US Geological Survey predicted that American oil reserves would run out in a few years. He advised the US government to take steps to secure new supplies from the Persian Gulf.

WRITING MYTH 1

You Can't Start a Sentence with *But*, *And* or *Because*

But you can. And you sometimes must. Because your writing will be punchy and powerful if you do. I know what you're thinking: 'But, Terry, when I was at Bash Street Primary School my teacher used to tell me off if I ever did this.' Primary school teachers do a difficult job, and they do it well. But I'm afraid I have to tell you that this is not really the whole truth.

Don't get bitter about this. Imagine your primary school teacher's predicament. As a five-year-old, you and all your friends in the class probably wrote like this (I've corrected your spelling mistakes):

And then we went on holiday. And then I had an ice cream. But Mummy and Daddy had a row. Because my little sister started crying. And then I went to bed.

Many of my friends still write that way. Seriously, primary school teachers get fed up with that sort of writing. So they try to get you to write longer sentences and use different 'joining' words. All power to their elbow. I think I might do the same in their shoes. But they mustn't start filling little heads with the idea that what is a sensible style guide (that is, don't begin every sentence with *but* or *and*) is a rule of grammar. Because it isn't.

Words such as *but*, *and*, *because* and *or* are what grammar books call **conjunctions**. This fancy word, of Latin origin, simply means 'to join with'. Conjunctions can join words to words, parts of sentences to other parts of sentences, and one sentence to another.

And Then There Was Light

A 'rule' that claimed we couldn't use conjunctions to begin sentences would make writing English almost impossible. None of these sentences, for instance, would be allowed:

While I was in Paris, I visited the Eiffel Tower.

When the going gets tough, the tough get going.

As my wife was ill, we didn't go to the theatre on Tuesday.

That's right: *while*, *when* and *as* are all conjunctions. And there are many others. If you've had no problem starting sentences with these words, then you can't logically object to starting a sentence with any conjunction. Indeed, I expect there is no word in English with which you could not, potentially, begin a sentence. But don't let me know if you think of one.

This is from a company's instructions to its customers about how to assemble a kitchen cooker hood. A very bad translation, you're thinking, but what language it was translated from we can only guess.

When you mount the cooker hood on a modulated kitchen, please care that the superior border of the calibre is on the inferior border of the incorporated kitchen. When you fix the cooker hood to the incorporated board, please set this border on the wall upon the bottom of the incorporated board et use the un-hooped holes.

Pick up those tools and get building!

A fear of putting a full stop before *and*, *but* and *because* will mean that you risk making your sentences too long. Or you will begin too many sentences with words such as *furthermore*, *additionally*, *nevertheless* and other multisyllable monstrosities.

You won't find a single grammar book that says anything about what words you can start a sentence with. And every great writer in English has quite freely started sentences with *and* and *but*: Daniel Defoe, Dr Johnson, the Brontë sisters, Jane Austen, Charles Dickens, Robert Louis Stevenson, George Orwell. And me!

We can start with one of the greatest works of English literature: the Authorised Version, or the 'King James Version', of the Bible. Published in 1611, it starts breaking the primary school 'rule' very early on: 'And God said let there be light. And there was light.' And if you've ever sung along with William Blake's 'Jerusalem' on the Last Night of the Proms then you've had no problem shouting out at the beginning, 'And did those feet in ancient time …' All right, stop singing.

A few years ago I spent a lot of money on the *Longman Comprehensive Grammar of the English Language*. Several pounds in weight, three inches thick, and 1,800 pages long, it was the best £99 I've ever spent. And, of course, I've read every word of it (almost). The four distinguished professors who compiled this masterpiece don't mention anything about a grammatical rule stopping us from beginning sentences with *and*, *but* and *because*. And they do so themselves on practically every page.

My last piece of evidence, your honour, is a quotation from that wonderful guide to clear writing: Sir Ernest Gowers's *The Complete Plain Words*. It was first published in 1954, with the aim of improving the writing standards of civil servants. It's been in print ever since. Gowers was a distinguished gentleman, who died in 1966. He was a well-educated man: Rugby School and Clare College, Cambridge, with a first-class honours degree in Classics – Greek and Latin to you. He was president of the English Association, and he had more honorary degrees than I've had hot dinners. This is what he says on page 98 of the paperback edition:

> There used to be an idea that it was inelegant to begin a sentence with *and*. The idea is now dead. And to use *and* in this position may be a useful way of indicating that what you are about to say will reinforce what you have just said. But do not do this so often that it becomes a mannerism. *But*, on the other hand, may be freely used to begin either a sentence or a paragraph.

Well said, Sir Ernest. He enjoyed writing that, didn't he? You can argue with him if you like. But I won't. Because he's right. And that's that.

GRAMMAR TIP 2
Are You Too Passive?

No, don't put on your tracksuit and trainers. You look reasonably fit. I mean, do you use the **passive voice** of the verb too often when you write? Puzzled? Well read on. By the end of this chapter you will have picked up one of the best techniques for improving your writing. The bad news is that writers who take their jobs seriously *must* know the difference between active and passive. The good news is that it's easy to learn.

Let's take a simple sentence:

The boy kicked the ball.

It should be easy to spot the **verb** (the 'doing word', as they call it at school). It's obviously *kicked*. But who's 'doing' the 'doing' word? Obviously, it's the boy. We call that person the **agent**. When we've got the agent before the verb, then we have the **active voice**.

What if I decide to start that sentence with 'The ball'? How would I have to carry on? That's right:

The ball was kicked by the boy.

Let's see what has happened. We've obviously got two verbs now: *was* (part of the verb *to be*) and *kicked*. But where's our agent? The boy has now moved after what he is doing. And when that happens we have the **passive**. Easy or not?

But you're thinking, 'What has this got to do with the price of fish?' Well, the passive has its uses, and we'll look at them in a minute. But the active has four major advantages:

1. **It gives information in the logical order.** Who is doing it, what they are doing, and what they are doing it to. We don't use the passive much when we speak. If I asked whether you were going to the office party and you replied, 'Terry, the party will not be attended by me,' I'd have you locked up.

2. **The active is more human.** There is a temptation in passive sentences to leave the agent out. You can often recognise a passive sentence because there is no human being in sight. Being impersonal can be useful sometimes, but if you do this too often your writing can seem cold and inhuman. And I'm sure you're not like that.

3. **The passive takes more words.** A paragraph with several passives can waste 25 to 30 words. A page of passives can contain 80 to 100 time wasters. Give me a four-page report that uses too many passives and I guarantee we can lose one page of the report if we rewrite it using mainly actives.

4. **You can cause ambiguity by using too many passives.** Some passive sentences have no agent in them. The reader may no longer know who should be doing something. They may guess the wrong agent.

I saw this notice in a hotel next to the lift (the notice was on every floor of the hotel, including the ground floor). Sensible advice, but what was the advice?

Please walk up one floor or down two for improved lift service.

Did you get it? Give in? I'll put you out of your misery. What it's really saying is: if you're going up only one floor, or down two floors, why don't you use the stairs instead of the lift, you lazy person!

Passive Hunting for Beginners

It's quite straightforward spotting passives. We can divide the process into three stages.

1. The first sign that you may have entered the passive zone (the 'twilight zone' of writing) is part of the verb *to be*. This will be one of eight words:

   am, is, was, were, are, be, been, being

2. The second sign is what we call (steady, now) the **past participle** of the verb. Don't panic. 'But, Terry, I wouldn't recognise the past participle if it came up and sat on me,' you're complaining. Finding the past participle of the verb is easy. For instance, *love* gives us the past participle *loved*; *consult* gives *consulted*; *decide* becomes *decided*; *choose* gives *chosen*; *drive* gives *driven*.

   This is simple, you're thinking: we just add *–d, –ed* or *–en* to the verb. But we have a few irregular past participles (we mustn't make English too easy to learn). However, you'll instinctively recognise the irregulars: *buy* becomes *bought*; *drink* becomes *drunk*; *seek* becomes *sought*; *slide* becomes *slid*; and so on. We even have a few verbs that don't change at all: *cut* and *hit*, for instance. We say *I cut*, *I was cut* or even *I had cut*. Be it regular or irregular, you'll have no trouble spotting a past participle when you meet one. You've been using them for years and never known.

3. Once we've got the part of the verb *to be* and the past participle, we can now go agent hunting. The agent may have disappeared from the sentence completely. But if the agent is present he, she, they (or occasionally it) will come after the word *by*.

We've got our three clues, so let's go passive hunting.

*The report **was sent** to the Finance Director **by** the Audit Office on 1 March 1999.*

In bold are the words that show a passive. Want to try again?

*Customers' opinions **were sought by** our Market Research Department.*

And one more for luck:

*The new salary scales had **been negotiated** in June 1999.*

Here we've lost the agent (either it obviously isn't important, or it's obvious to the reader), but we still have a passive, because we've got the other two elements: part of the verb *to be* (in this case, *been*), and the past participle *negotiated*.

When you write, try to keep about 75 per cent of your verbs active. Your writing will soon become more direct and more human. Notice how much sharper your writing becomes when you use mainly active verbs. Let's put into the active the two sentences we used as examples:

The Audit Office sent the report to the Finance Director on 1 March 1999.

Our Market Research Department sought customers' opinions.

Four words lost in the rewrite. And that's in just two sentences. We keep *sent* and *sought* in our active versions, but we can dump the parts of the verb *to be* and the *by*.

There's a Time to be Passive

The passive has its uses. Three, to be precise. It can 'soften' bad news:

ACTIVE:
We will evict you on 10 March if you do not pay the rent.

PASSIVE:
*You will **be evicted** on 10 March if the rent **is** not **paid**.*

The passive version does not say who will evict or who should pay the rent. It's softer, but the active might get the rent paid! I'd use the passive if they owe you one week's rent, but the active if they owe you a lot.

The second use of the passive (and a questionable one) is avoiding responsibility:

ACTIVE:
We have mislaid your papers.

PASSIVE:
*Your papers have **been mislaid**.*

Unless you have a good reason for not stating clearly who has 'mislaid' the papers, I wouldn't use this type of passive too much. It will simply annoy your readers even more. They're not fools (we hope). But the passive can be useful if it's the customer who makes the mistake:

*Unfortunately, the form **was filled** in incorrectly.*

This sounds more polite than with the agent put in:

Unfortunately, you filled the form in incorrectly.

The third use of the passive is to focus on the person receiving the action of the verb. Putting the agent to the rear can be sensible sometimes, and is particularly effective in headlines for newspapers or newsletters:

ACTIVE:
Bloxwich Council has evicted twenty tenants for rent arrears this year.

PASSIVE:
*Twenty tenants **are evicted** for rent arrears this year (**by** Bloxwich Council).*

I've put the *by Bloxwich Council* in parentheses because we could possibly leave it out if the agent was obvious from the context (this might be a headline from the *Bloxwich Council Newsletter*, for instance). Journalists are a bit naughty and tend to leave out the part of the verb *to be* in headlines: *Twenty tenants evicted for rent arrears*. That will do for a headline, but we can't always do it in normal business writing.

One last thing. If you write on a computer you'll find that many word-processing programs spot some passives when they do a grammar check. The bad news is that they miss quite a few, so you can't rely on your computer to do all the work. You mustn't be too passive!

Exercise: Gain from Pain

Underline the passives in the following sentences, then rewrite all of them as actives. You will need to change the word order, obviously, but don't change the meaning.

1. The bid was submitted by Taylor Investments after the closing date.

2. The recommendations of the personnel manager were accepted by the board of directors.

3. The presentation will be made, and the key problems will be highlighted, by Sarah Clark, our Production Manager.

4. New staff are often baffled by the complexity of our accounts system and their work efficiency is reduced.

5. An application form is enclosed. All sections should be completed and returned by 25 May. Your application will be considered and you will be informed of our decision as soon as possible.

   (Tip: This is from a local council's letter to a resident. Try to make it more personal when you change the passives into actives. You will have to bring in the human agents.)

Possible Rewrites

1. Taylor Investments submitted the bid after the closing date. (Passive: *was submitted*.)

2. The board of directors accepted the recommendations of the personnel manager. (Passive: *were accepted*.)

3. Sarah Clark, our Production Manager, will make the presentation and highlight the key problems. (Passives: *be made* and *be highlighted*.)

4. The complexity of our accounts system often baffles new staff and reduces their work efficiency. (Passives: *are baffled* and *is reduced*.)

5. I enclose an application form. You should fill in all sections and return it by 25 May. We will consider your application and let you know our decision as soon as possible. (Passives: *is enclosed*, *be completed*, *(be) returned*, *be considered*, and *be informed*.)

WRITING MYTH 2
It's Wrong to *Boldly* Go

Do we have any *Star Trek* fans in the audience? If so, they'll be familiar, whether they realise it or not, with the most famous split infinitive in the language (or the universe): '… to boldly go where no man has gone before'. 'What's wrong with that?' you might ask (apart from the obviously sexist 'man').

Well, grammatical cranks, for a hundred years or so, have been trying to convince us that it's wrong to split the **infinitive** of the verb. And what is the infinitive of the verb? Here are a few infinitives for you to studiously pore over (did you spot that split infinitive?):

to see, to laugh, to go, to march, to exploit

I think you've got the picture by now. So our cranky friends say it's wrong to put a word between the two words of the infinitive:

to quickly see

to loudly laugh

to boldly go

to proudly march

to creatively exploit

to studiously pore

Words such as *quickly*, *loudly*, *boldly*, *proudly*, and *creatively* are **adverbs**. They add information about the verb. The verb tells us what we are doing, and the adverb tells us in what way we are doing it. So why shouldn't we put adverbs anywhere we like so long as it is quite clear which verb we are adding information to?

The 'rule' against splitting infinitives is nonsense. And dangerous nonsense, because trying to avoid splitting the infinitive can sometimes make our sentences ambiguous:

The policeman was forced reluctantly to arrest the suspect.

Does this mean that PC Plod was reluctant to arrest the suspect? Or does it mean that the people who forced him to arrest Burglar Bill were reluctant to do so? If it means the first, then *to reluctantly arrest* gets rid of the ambiguity.

And avoiding the split infinitive can make our sentences awkward:

The enemy continues heavily to outnumber [or to outnumber heavily] *our troops.*

This would seem far more natural as:

The enemy continues to heavily outnumber our troops.

We would certainly say it that way. In fact, we split infinitives quite naturally when we speak. But the minute we write one the language police will dive in with their red pens and smirks of superiority. Because some people have no other role in life but to spot (to *gleefully* spot?) split infinitives. It's in their job description. They may not know another single 'rule' of grammar but they will enforce this non-rule. They probably think that split infinitives were the real cause of the fall of the British Empire.

Where did this nonsense come from? From the ancient Romans, no less. In Latin, take my word for it, the infinitive was (usually) one word. So you couldn't split an infinitive even if you took a pickaxe to it. I'm all for learning Latin. But what worked for Julius Caesar in Ancient Rome probably won't work for you and me in 2006.

Someone wrote to their local public library asking if they could put up some posters advertising community events. This is part of the reply they received from the librarian.

Your enquiry about the use of the entrance area of the library for displaying posters gives rise to the question of the provenance and authoritativeness of the material to be displayed ... Items of a disputatious or polemic kind, whilst not necessarily excluded, are considered individually.

What's your problem? You've got a dictionary, haven't you? In case you can't find a dictionary handy, I think what the librarian is saying is, 'We've got to have a look at them first.' I don't think this librarian will be stocking my book.

To Infinitives and Beyond

Perhaps we're all making a fuss over nothing. It's usually quite possible to rewrite a sentence if you don't want to upset the split infinitive police. But perhaps we should all throw in the odd one just to annoy them. Remember what the great Raymond Chandler (author of *The Big Sleep*, *Farewell, My Lovely*, and many other fine suspense novels) said when an editor once had the nerve to tell him that he had spotted a split infinitive in a Chandler manuscript: 'When I split an infinitive, God damn it, I split it so it will stay split!' And Chandler went to the exclusive Dulwich College.

Time to quickly beam me up, Scottie.

GRAMMAR TIP 3
Be Commanding

This is where we need to put a bit of (to use a little management jargon) 'assertiveness training' into your language. You're going to learn now about the **imperative mood** of the verb. I bet you thought that only teenage children had moods, didn't you? Well, I'm afraid I have to tell you that English verbs have moods as well. Three, to be precise.

1. The Indicative Mood

We use this verb mood to state facts or ask questions. We're 'indicating' facts:

*He **drives** to work on Monday.*

*Terry **worked** very hard.*

***Is** Mary in the house?*

2. The Subjunctive Mood

We use this mood (rarely these days) for wishes, conditions or possibilities. Lawyers still love the subjunctive!

*The agreement stated that Mr Clark **pay** [not pays] his rent regularly.*

*If I **were** [not was] you, I wouldn't do that.*

*It is a strict requirement that he **attend** [not attends] court on 20 June.*

Now that you've learnt about the indicative and subjunctive moods you can instantly forget them. Gosh, I am being commanding, aren't I? The only mood that you'll really find useful to know about is the **imperative mood**. This is the mood that we use to give orders and instructions:

***Find** the Accounts Manager for me.*

***Stand** in the corner.*

***Phone** Dave on Saturday morning.*

***March** or die!*

All you have to do to find the imperative mood of a verb is to write out the form of the verb that takes *to* before it (the infinitive) and then drop the *to*:

to speak   gives us the imperative **speak**

| *to talk* | gives us the imperative **talk** |
| *to swim* | gives us the imperative **swim** |

Easy, isn't it? Put the verb to the front of the sentence and off we go. Office writers don't use the imperative mood enough. Use it more! It saves words, and what saves words saves time and my patience. Procedure manuals, assembly guides and instruction booklets contain too many of this sort of sentence:

The extension arm should be fitted to the unit.

This is ambiguous. Do you mean that the extension arm will already be on the unit? No, you probably mean that the reader should fit it. It is also too wordy. Let's use the imperative instead. What's the main verb here? Obviously it is *fitted*. *To fit* gives us the imperative *fit*. Let's try it:

Fit the extension arm to the unit.

Your colleagues, staff and customers want procedures and instructions that are short, clear and unambiguous. Use the imperative if you want to keep them happy. The odd 'please' thrown in (not too many) will make sure that no one will be upset by your new commanding tone. Anyway, your readers will probably be too busy racing through your new streamlined procedures and instructions to notice.

Who's Giving the Orders Here?

Of course, be careful where you use the imperative. It could come over as rather sharp in a letter to a customer or supplier, for instance. But in any piece of writing where your main job is to give a lot of instructions or information in a punchy and lively way it's your best friend. This is one mood you should indulge.

Now you can get into a grumpy mood, because it's exercise time again. Pick up that pen. And *that* was an imperative!

Exercise: Gain from Pain

Put the verbs in the following sentences into the imperative mood.

1. After you have completed the invoice form, the accounts manager should be sent a copy.

2. The stabiliser must be fitted securely to the rear axle.

3. All orders taken that day should be faxed through to head office before 5 PM.

4. All personnel files will be retained by you for two years.

5. Upon arrival at our office, make sure your name is given to the receptionist.

Possible Rewrites

The imperative mood verbs are in bold.

1. **Complete** the invoice form and **send** the accounts manager a copy.

2. **Fit** the stabiliser securely to the rear axle. Or: **Secure** the stabiliser to the rear axle.

3. **Fax** all that day's orders to head office before 5 PM.

4. **Retain** (or **Keep**) all personnel files for two years.

5. Please **give** your name to the receptionist when you arrive at our office.

Newspaper headline writers have to be concise. But some headlines take it too far. This is a headline from the medical pages of a local newspaper.

Prostate cancer more common in men

And on page 3: 'Pregnancy problems more common in women'?

WRITING MYTH 3
Get, Getting and Got Aren't Proper Words

I edit as well as teach to pay the mortgage. When I'm editing, I sometimes see the most amazingly obscure, or pretentious, word, chosen from the very wildest edges of the thesaurus, and I think, 'What you really mean here, my friend, is the word *got*, *get* or *getting*.' Why do so many office writers have a strange fear of writing these words?

You get up in the morning, get dressed, get breakfast, get on the train, get off the train, and get to work on time (we hope). But when you start writing in the office you tell me you can't use *get*. This is getting ridiculous.

Yet again, I suspect primary school teachers may be responsible for this. Even I remember that once a week in primary school our teacher would write on the blackboard 'Better words'. Underneath that the teacher would write:

I got six presents on my birthday.

A sentence that I could see no problem with at all. 'Well, class,' the teacher would say, 'I'm sure little Terence can think of a better word than *got* in that sentence.' And little Terence would shake his blond mop and reply, 'No, I can't.' That's what I thought, anyway.

I think my primary teacher should have written on the board 'Different words'. Because the teacher was really trying to increase our vocabulary, given that children overuse the words *got* and *get*. A laudable aim, because we don't want to use the verb *to get* all the time. Or to use *get* when it's a lazy substitute for a better verb. But we mustn't start thinking that we can't write the words in polite company without provoking a shocked outburst from the reader. Presumably the teacher wanted:

I was in receipt of six presents on my birthday.

Ridiculous. And don't forget the Bible: Proverbs 4, verse 7 (as I'm sure you knew):

Wisdom is the principal thing, therefore get wisdom and with all thy getting get understanding.

Poetry I call that. You can imagine the average office writer editing that sentence:

Wisdom is the main and principal thing, therefore be in receipt of wisdom and with all thine obtaining be in further receipt of understanding.

I don't know about you, but that version doesn't do a lot for me. I'll stick with the Authorised Version.

> These instructions for assembling a chair take a commendably direct approach to the problems of life.
>
> `Assemble the single parts (see picture) following nrs 1-2-3. Insert the wheels in the prepared holes in the base. If the wheels are provided with filleted pins, screw them.`
>
> I know the feeling.

Get Off

Train announcers amuse me. Trains never 'leave', but they always 'depart'. They never have a 'final stop', but they 'terminate'. But the words they really can't say are 'get on' and 'get off'. Passengers 'board' and 'alight'. The 'alight' one really tickles me. No one has 'alighted' from a moving object since Jane Austen's time. American tourists must think it's time to start smoking.

We use the words *get*, *got* and *getting* quite naturally and politely when we are talking to colleagues or customers. If you think you could use one of these words in a perfectly grammatical way if you were speaking to someone, then don't be frightened of writing it occasionally. They will make your writing natural and human. You can *get* a letter or a report, you don't have to be *in receipt of* it. There are lots of other good verbs to use if we think we are using *get* or *got* too often: *obtain*, *receive* and so on. But we mustn't have a blanket ban on using the most obvious word at times. Get a life!

GRAMMAR TIP 4
The 'Doing' Word and What to Do with It

I've been rude about your old primary school teacher. But the teacher probably gave you one useful piece of grammatical information that you will remember: the verb is the 'doing word'. And you won't ever come up with a better definition. The verb is the doing word: it does the really valuable work in language. The verb is the motor that moves our ideas. Good writers use verbs well. Bad writers don't. Bad writers do this:

> *They make poor utilisation of verbs, by the conversion of many verbs into nouns.*

Horrible sentence, isn't it? Want to know why? The writer is doing something common in bad writing: turning words that could have been powerful verbs into nouns. *Use* becomes *utilisation*, *convert* becomes *conversion*.

And then the bad writer has to bring in other verbs to get the sentences rolling along, so the waffle starts coming in as well. Let's look at that sentence again. I've underlined the verbs and put the nouns in bold:

They <u>make</u> poor **utilisation** of **verbs**, by the **conversion** of many **verbs** into **nouns**.

There are five nouns and just one verb. Notice the heaviness and wordiness of this writing. We could have done better. We obviously need the nouns *verbs* and *nouns*. But let's do something with *utilisation* and *conversion*. Because if we look closely we can see that there are verbs hidden in them:

They <u>use</u> **verbs** poorly, by <u>converting</u> many **verbs** into **nouns**.

We've nearly halved the noun count, and reduced the sentence from 14 words to 10. And notice how the new sentence runs instead of crawls.

You may be surprised that words such as *utilisation* and *conversion* are nouns. But they are. If you remember any more school grammar, you may remember how your teacher defined the noun: a 'thing word'. If you think about nouns at all (and be honest, you probably go weeks without thinking about nouns), you think of things you can touch and see: book, pen, car, house and so on.

If you compare 'decision' with 'book', you can see how grammatically similar they are. You can put 'the' or 'a' in front of them. You can make them plurals in the same way: *decisions, books.* You can own them: *my decision, my book.* You can even use an apostrophe with them: *the decision's impact, the book's pages.* Like it or not, 'decision' and 'book' are both nouns.

My neighbour left me a letter trying to get some work for his cleaner, Isabella. I'm not sure Isabella will get many job offers.

`Isabella has worked as my cleaner for a number of months. She is terrific both at cleaning and at washing and ironing and is wholly trustworthy. She is exceptionally contentious.`

A 'contentious' cleaner? That's a cleaner who says, 'Clean that yourself, I'm not doing it!' I'm actually looking for a *conscientious* cleaner.

Don't be Abstracted

In fact, there's an important class of nouns called **abstract nouns**. Words such as *agreement, decision* and *analysis* are abstract nouns. They describe an activity or idea. They are nouns, but not the ones you can see and touch.

But look closely and you'll see that *agreement, decision* and *analysis* are nouns that hide verbs: *to agree, to decide, to analyse.* You must reveal your hidden verbs. So don't write sentences like these:

*Management and workers reached an **agreement** to meet every three months.*

*The Bank of England made the **decision** to raise interest rates by 1 per cent.*

*Professor Brainstorm conducted an **analysis** of the data in November 1999.*

I'm sure you're thinking that you can do better. And you can (revealed verbs in bold):

*Management and workers **agreed** to meet every three months.*

*The Bank of England **decided** to raise interest rates by 1 per cent.*

*Professor Brainstorm **analysed** the data in November 1999.*

You've simply revealed the verbs tucked under the abstract nouns. Once again, you've given the sentences a bit of life, and saved on toner.

The Verb is the Word

An abstract noun that hides a verb is a **nominalisation**. Horrible word, I know. I only put it in to impress you.

But I'm sure you've got the idea by now, so I won't mention it again. I promise.

We can't do without some abstract nouns. But too many will slow your writing down and add waffle. There's a third reason to avoid them: they often drag passive verbs in their wake, and you lose the last lingering touch of humanity in your writing. Look at these sentences (abstract nouns in bold, passives underlined):

*An **agreement** <u>was reached</u> to meet every three months.*

*The **decision** <u>was made</u> to raise interest rates by 1 per cent.*

*An **analysis** of the data <u>was conducted</u> in November 1999.*

Slow, wordy and impersonal – three strikes and you're out.

So, if your writing seems heavy, look for abstract nouns that you can turn into verbs. A couple of clues will help you. Certain endings are common when you turn a verb into a noun:

decide	*deci**sion***
agree	*agree**ment***
waste	*wast**age***
refuse	*refus**al***
amaze	*amaze**ment***

The *-ion* ending is particularly common. And abstract nouns usually attract little words either side, which is why they lead to waffle. The little words are often *the*, *an*, or *a* at the start (the **articles**), and a **preposition** (such as *of, from, to, in, into*) at the end. The abstract noun becomes the middle part of a sandwich, a sandwich that grammarians call, unappetisingly, a 'noun phrase'.

the decision to

an analysis of

the removal of

a refusal from

a conversion into

with reference to

Office Clichés

Certain abstract nouns appear too often in office writing, usually doing nothing much. No one is banning them, but use them only when you need to. I'm sure you can rewrite all these examples without using the nouns in bold. Why don't you, then?

*The company agreed to limited exploration **activity**.*

*They accepted employment on a part-time **basis**.*

*The delegate said the claims were of a far-reaching **character**.*

*Better economic **conditions** will prevail in the spring.*

*The problem is of a considerable **extent**.*

*Another **issue** concerning the association is the problem of staff retention.*

*Building **operations** have been going on for over a year.*

*The director said that the staffing **position** would then be reviewed.*

*Over the **question** of supply, the major decision in the near future will be purchasing new computers.*

Exercise: Gain from Pain

Rewrite these sentences so that you reveal the verbs hidden beneath nouns.

1. The new job descriptions will help in the motivation of staff.

2. The consultants recommended the reorganisation of the IT Department and the creation of four posts.

3. Acceptance of the new process by staff was made easier with the introduction of the new salary scales.

4. Defect avoidance and an increase in productivity were essential requirements.

5. The committee voted for the expulsion of several members and the removal of their names from the professional register.

6. The engineers paid a visit to our Norwich factory, and made several suggestions about improvements to production procedures.

Possible Rewrites

The revealed verbs are in bold.

1. The new job descriptions will help **motivate** staff.

2. The consultants recommended **reorganising** the IT department and **creating** four posts.

3. Staff **accepted** the new process more easily when new salary scales were **introduced**.

4. **Avoiding** defects and **increasing** productivity were essential requirements.

5. The committee voted to **expel** several members and **remove** their names from the professional register.

6. The engineers **visited** our Norwich factory and **suggested** several improvements to production procedures.

WRITING MYTH 4
Positioning Your Prepositions

You may be in the relatively happy position of not knowing what a **preposition** is. In which case I'm going to have to lighten your dark ignorance. A preposition is a word we put before a noun or a pronoun and which shows a connection. Sounds a bit technical? Some simple examples will make it clear (prepositions in bold):

in the building

on the table

to the shop

The English language is full of prepositions (other examples: *for, with, by, from, over, at*), and useful they are. English without prepositions would sound something like:

Take me your leader. I have arrived Mars. Can you direct me a petrol station? I have run out rocket fuel.

Not a pretty sight, I'm sure you will agree. Even good old ET could surely have managed:

*Take me **to** your leader. I have arrived **from** Mars. Can you direct me **to** a petrol station? I have run out **of** rocket fuel.*

So I'm all for prepositions. But I'm not for silly so-called rules about prepositions.

The most misleading 'rule' is that you shouldn't end a sentence with a preposition. This rule was, once again, derived from Latin. Trying to apply the rules of a strait-laced language such as Latin to an essentially freewheeling language such as English has caused too much trouble. What sounds good in Latin sounds daft in English. For instance (prepositions in bold):

*Who was your appointment **with**?*

is surely preferable to the rather stuffy

***With** whom was your appointment?*

And this perfectly natural sentence:

*This is a problem the company could really do **without**.*

sounds less awkward than the so-called correct

*This is a problem **without** which the company could really do.*

And many verbs in English are what we call **phrasal verbs**. This means that they have a preposition attached to the main part of the verb. For example, *come about*, *draw up*, *put up with*, *work out*. I don't know about you, but 'A taxi drew up' seems more natural to me than 'Up drew a taxi.'

Let your ear do the writing (a difficult way to hold the pen, I know). In other words, put the preposition where it sounds natural. And if that is at the end of the sentence, then leave it there. When some officious jobsworth tried to correct something that Winston Churchill had written that ended with a preposition, Churchill wrote back, 'This is one rule up with which I will not put.' Although Winnie never went so far as to say, 'We shall fight them the beaches on.' Winnie knew when the preposition sounded silly at the end of a sentence. He used his ears. And you should use yours.

Am I Too Complex?

While we're on the subject of prepositions, good writers always prefer the simple preposition (and the simple conjunction) to the complex preposition (or conjunction). I give you some examples of both:

Complex phrases	Simple words
prior to	*before*
subsequent to	*after*
previous to	*before*
in the event of (that)	*if, when*
in the vicinity of	*near*
in the course of	*during*
in accordance with	*by, under, because of*
for the duration of	*while*
with regard to	*about, concerning*
in conjunction with	*and, with*
for the purpose of	*to, for*
with effect from	*from*

There are many more examples. The occasional complex preposition (between consenting adults) won't do any harm. But don't get into the habit of using them. The simple prepositions are more natural. Too many complex prepositions will make your writing starchy, wordy and clumsy.

Health advice is always useful. But I'm not sure about this sign I saw in a health clinic.

For Birth Control, please use rear entrance.

Words failed the writer, and words fail me.

I was editing a company's customer contract a short time ago. The writer had lost that part of his brain that could use the word *if* or *when*, but used instead *in the event of* or *in the event that* 42 times in four pages. You don't need a calculator to work out that that comes out to more than 100 redundant words. The first thing customers do when they get this sort of contract is to check how long it is. Why not make the information as concise as possible? So use a simple preposition where you can.

By the way, I always say to writers who use *prior to* for *before* too often, 'I expect you use *posterior to* for afterwards.' And sometimes a mad look of triumph comes into their eyes, and I can see them thinking, 'No, but I will in future!'

And remember not to add a preposition to a verb that is doing the job adequately on its own. None of the prepositions in these sentences is doing anything for human progress (prepositions in bold):

*We need to meet **up** next Tuesday and consult **with** the sales staff.*

*You need to check **up on** the sales figures for last month and then test **out** the new procedures.*

Being concise *pays*, it doesn't have to *pay off*.

GRAMMAR TIP 5

Adjectives and How to Avoid Them

English would be dull without adjectives. How else could I describe your many qualities? *Handsome, intelligent, graceful, talented, loyal*: words that spring to the lips of your friends every day. Of course, behind your back, I could be telling the truth about you: *plain, stupid, clumsy, talentless, fickle*. But, whether I'm being truthful or lying, I've got to use **adjectives**. That's right, the words in italics are adjectives. We use them to describe things (nouns). Not just to give things qualities, but shapes, colours, ages and so on. All of the words in bold in the following are adjectives:

the **old** man

the sky is **blue**

*the **loud** noise*

*the board is **square***

*the **laughing** policeman*

So why do I want to avoid adjectives when they're doing such fine work? Because too many adjectives are pointless and account for much of the waffle in bad writing. 'The adjective is too often the parasite sucking life from language,' one genius wrote. Actually, I just made that up. But it's true.

The first misuse of adjectives is when the adjective is doing nothing that the noun can't do on its own. Look at these common examples (adjectives in bold):

*a **general** consensus*	(A consensus is a *general* agreement.)
*a **component** part*	(Use either *component* or *part*, not both.)
*a **terrible** disaster*	(Are there *non-terrible* disasters?)
*our **future** plans*	(How can you plan for anything but the future?)
*a **safe** haven*	(No such thing as a *dangerous* haven.)
***new** innovation*	(What's the *new* doing?)
***free** gift*	(All true gifts are free.)

The adjective and the noun are holding hands in such cases. But we have to separate the little friends. The noun is big enough to stand on its own, and it doesn't need the adjective to help it along.

Two for the Price of One

In this class we can include office clichés, such as 'a real danger' (would I be interested in imaginary ones?), or 'a puzzling question' (don't questions generally puzzle you?), or a 'viable solution' (please don't bother me with the nonviable ones).

The second type of wasted adjective appears when the writer can't trust one adjective to do the job and brings on another that simply repeats the first. Some examples (adjectives once again in bold):

a **clear** and **distinct** *view*

a **key** and **important** *decision*

a **strange** and **remarkable** *event*

a **remote** and **isolated** *cottage*

Lawyers are especially fond of this doubling up of words: 'each and every', 'null and void', 'over and above', 'full and final'. There's a wicked rumour that lawyers used to get paid by the word. It's not true: they get paid by the second.

The third poor use of adjectives comes when they are hiding a verb. The following examples are typical of old-fashioned 'office' writing (adjectives in bold):

*The survey is **indicative** that our customers are **supportive** of our restructuring.*

*I am **dubious** that all of the factors are **applicable** in this case.*

The ponderous adjectives in this sort of writing nearly always follow part of the verb *to be*: *am, is, was, were, are, be, been, being.* A word ending in *-ive, -ous, -able* or *-ible* often shows an adjective hiding a verb. Don't hide the action in this way, but replace the adjectives with verbs (in bold):

*The survey **indicates** that customers **support** our restructuring.*

*I **doubt** that all of the factors **apply** in this case.*

Beware in particular of overusing certain 'office' adjectives: *key, major, focused, essential, crucial, upcoming, ongoing* and the like. Once, when the world was young and we were beautiful (well I was), these adjectives no doubt had a spring in their step. Nowadays, like me, they limp along like geriatric, timeworn relics. Time to put them out of their misery where possible. Be cruel to adjectives and you'll be kind to language.

You're Too Intense

Another common problem with adjectives is placing before them a pointless **intensifier**. Intensifiers are words such as *very, most, really, totally*. *Very*, for instance, is a (very) overused word in flabby office writing. Look at these examples (intensifiers in bold):

a **very** *important obligation*

a **most** *unusual event*

a **really** *innovative suggestion*

a **totally** *honest employee*

an **undoubtedly** *powerful argument*

The adjectives doing the useful work here are *important, unusual, innovative, honest, powerful*. The intensifiers aren't adding much. We're saving only a word each time if we take them out, but you'd be surprised how these wasted words add up. No one's going to ban you from using the occasional intensifier, if you *really* need it. But don't overdo them. Less can be more.

Exercise: Gain from Pain

Red-pen time again. Chop out the redundant adjectives and intensifiers in the following sentences, or replace the adjectives with verbs.

1. The results are illustrative of the fact that our customers are appreciative of our efforts.

2. John was fearful of failure, while Mike was hopeful of success.

3. He really was a most talented sculptor, and had made an exact replica of Michelangelo's *David*.

4. The castle is a very unique attraction, and its former history is extremely fascinating.

5. In my personal opinion a driving test is an essential condition before employing Mr Davis.

6. The final outcome of the meeting was the introduction of new amended and modified safety procedures.

Possible Rewrites

1. The results illustrate that our customers appreciate our efforts.

2. John feared failure, while Mike hoped for success.

3. He was a talented sculptor, and had made a replica of Michelangelo's *David*.

4. The castle is unique, and its history is fascinating.

5. In my opinion a driving test is essential before employing Mr Davis.

6. The outcome of the meeting was the introduction of amended safety procedures.

'Management speak' often means well, but sometimes you just wish it would get to the point. This extract from a management magazine article on 'organisational culture' brings a warm glow to my heart, and a tear to my eye.

The strength of a culture depends on three things; first, the pervasiveness of the norms and behaviours in the explicit culture, and the pervasiveness of the values and beliefs in the implicit culture — ie the proportion of the members of the social group that firmly hold to the norms and beliefs. Secondly, cultural strength depends on the pervasiveness of the beliefs and behaviours themselves — ie the range of behaviours and the range of beliefs and values which the culture sets out to control.

I think they should set that to music.

WRITING MYTH 5
You Cannot Use *Can't*

I'm going to be talking about **contractions** in this chapter. Don't worry, ladies, we won't be back in the maternity ward. I'm not talking about the sort of contraction that comes at the end of nine months but the sort that comes at the beginning of this sentence: *I'm*. Short for, as if you didn't know, *I am*.

There is a persistent belief that contractions are not acceptable in 'proper' business writing, and that they are 'ungrammatical'. An attitude that can damage your writing. Using contracted forms occasionally – *don't*, *can't*, *that's*, *it's* and so on – can make your writing natural and flowing. So we shouldn't (or should not?) turn our noses up at them.

Many language fogies think that contractions are a nasty modern development. In fact, most of them have been around a long time. The *Oxford English Dictionary*, for instance, gives 1660 for the first appearance of *won't*,

1670 for *don't*, 1706 for *can't*, and 1836 for *wouldn't*. They've been among us for a few years. We should be used to them by now.

They're such a normal part of modern English that the full forms of some contractions now sound unnatural in most situations. For instance, 'I can't explain' is almost universal, except in cases of real emphasis, when we might use 'I *cannot* explain.'

Undoubtedly, some contractions are more usual than others. But I do think we could generally use the following common contractions when writing in the office, unless the document is *very* formal.

it's	it is or it has	*can't*	cannot
isn't	is not	*won't*	will not
they've	they have	*doesn't*	does not
you've	you have	*couldn't*	could not
we've	we have	*shouldn't*	should not
they'd	they had	*wouldn't*	would not
you'd	you had	*shan't*	shall not
we're	we are	*mustn't*	must not
they're	they are	*where's*	where is or where has
you're	you are	*that's*	that is

I'll	*I will*	*he's*	*he is* or *he has*
I'm	*I am*	*she's*	*she is* or *she has*
we'll	*we will*	*there's*	*there is* or *there has*
you'll	*you will*	*here's*	*here is*
they'll	*they will*	*now's*	*now is*
aren't	*are not*	*who's*	*who is* or *who has*

There's no need to use the contraction every time you write. Just because you wrote *they're* at the top of the page, it doesn't mean you can't use *they are* at the bottom. And you must always be conscious of the tone you are trying to achieve in a document. What might be acceptable in an email to a colleague might not be acceptable in a formal company report or an insurance policy. Using contracted forms is also subject to fashion and stylistic change (*ain't*, for instance, used to be quite socially acceptable – it ain't now). But, generally, prefer the conversational to the stuffy.

Read the Contract

When you use contractions you must get the apostrophes right, even in the most informal document. There is no such word as *dont* in educated writing. And you must be exceptionally careful with these four contractions:

you're (short for *you are*. Don't confuse with *your*)

it's (short for *it is* or *it has*. Don't confuse with *its*)

who's (short for *who is* or *who has*. Don't confuse with *whose*)

let's (short for *let us*. Don't confuse with *lets*)

If you're in any doubt about which one of these to use, try the sentence with the full form of the contraction. If the full form sounds ridiculous, you know you've made a mistake. For instance, you might be tempted to write:

Who's book is this on the table?

Well don't give in to temptation. *Who's* is short for *who is* or *who has*. That's not what we are saying here. So we want the other one:

Whose book is this on the table?

Follow exactly the same rule for *it's*. Have a look at this sentence:

The cat licks it's paws.

Are we really saying *The cat licks it is paws*? No, we are not. So obviously the correct version is:

The cat licks its paws.

Confusing *it's* with *its* (or even inventing complete

rubbish such as *its'*) is one of the commonest errors of sloppy writers. So make sure you get this one right every time – it's important.

Here's another incorrect sentence:

Your not getting any younger, are you?

Unfortunately, your grammar isn't getting any better as you get older. Because what we are really saying here is *You are not getting*. So either we can use the two words *you are*, or we could contract them and correctly write:

You're not getting any younger, are you?

One last mistake:

She let's us leave early on Friday.

That's nice of her. But she will start keeping you in if you can't get your spelling right. *Let's* is a contraction of *let us*. So you are really saying here that *She let us us leave early*. Nonsense once again. What you want here is *lets*:

She lets us leave early on Friday.

Or:

Let's leave early on Friday, whether she agrees or not.

You might get in trouble for leaving early, but not for incorrect spelling. *Let's* in that sentence really does stand for *let us*.

Use contractions, therefore, especially when you want

a human, conversational style. But make sure when you do use them that you spell them correctly and that you use the right one.

While we are on the subject of contractions and abbreviations, let's look at three you should never go near unless you are pushed for space or time: *e.g.*, *i.e.* and *etc.* These are an abomination nowadays. Most writers no longer know what they are abbreviating (they are Latin: *exempli gratia*, *id est* and *et cetera*). They are too often misused and confused, often superfluous, and not always understood if you are writing for a wide audience. Prefer the English: *for example*, *in other words*, and *and so on*. Wonderful language Latin, and I'm glad I studied some at school. But the last Roman legion left Britannia about AD 410 (that's one Latin abbreviation I can live with). I believe they travelled on the evening ferry from Dover. They bought a single ticket and won't be coming back (I hope). So use English wherever you can.

Where would we be without credit cards? It's always useful when your bank explains how credit works.

The Principal Cardholder must repay at least 5 per cent of the amount shown on the statement as outstanding or £10 (or the full amount if less than £10), whichever is greater, within 25 days of the statement date (or, if the Bank considers that it is for any reason impossible or impractical to provide or send a statement, from the date determined by the Bank in accordance with condition 18), Condition 4.)

On second thoughts, I'll pay cash.

GRAMMAR TIP 6

Chopping Off Your Unwanted Auxiliaries

Don't worry, you don't need any medical knowledge to remove unwanted auxiliaries, just some grammatical information about verbs.

English has a simple grammar in many ways. This shows itself in our verbs. Other languages continually make changes to the ends of their verbs. To learn just the future **tense** of a French verb you have to memorise six different endings. But English is simplicity itself. No wonder we find foreign languages difficult! Most English regular verbs (and the majority of English verbs are polite enough to be regular) have just four forms to cover all the tenses: present, future and past. Take the verb *to love.* Here are its four forms:

love, loves, loving, loved

Even the irregular verbs in English usually get by with just five forms:

drive, drives, driving, drove, driven

Instead of playing about too much with the endings of its verbs, English likes to bring in helpful little words, called **auxiliary verbs**, to show distinctions of time and certainty. They come before the main verb. Here are some examples (auxiliaries in bold, main verbs underlined):

I **am** <u>writing</u> to Peter today.

I **have** <u>spoken</u> to Joanna.

I **had** <u>written</u> to Peter many times.

They **do** not <u>smoke</u>.

We **will be** <u>contacting</u> all our customers.

You **were** <u>driving</u> too fast.

They **could have** <u>replied</u> earlier.

They **might** <u>speak</u> to me.

The main auxiliary verbs are *to be*, *to have* and *to do*. Others are *can, could, may, might, will, would, shall, should, must*. The second group can't function as main verbs. The first group can:

*I **have** a car.*	(*Have* is a main verb.)
*I **have** bought a new car.*	(*Have* is an auxiliary verb to the main verb *bought*.)
*He **is** intelligent.*	(*Is* is a main verb.)
*He **is** reading more books.*	(*Is* is an auxiliary verb to the main verb *reading*.)

We often use auxiliary verbs to show at what time the action of the verb is happening. We call this **tense**. There are present, past and future tenses in English. Some examples for you:

Present tense	*I love, he loves, she is loving*
Simple past tense	*she loved, you loved, they loved*
Complex past tense	*I had loved, you have loved, they had been loving*
Future tense	*I shall love, we will love*

Given that English has a relatively simple verb system, we can't do without auxiliary verbs. But as good writers we can make sure that we don't use them when we don't need to. Generally, wherever you can, use the present or simple past tense of the verb. Don't be fanatical about this. But when you are pushed for space, or you need to do some extra sharp editing, amputating unnecessary auxiliary verbs is useful. Look at the following examples (auxiliary verbs in bold):

*We **are** employing six regional managers, and we **are** planning to appoint four more soon.*

*Sheila **has been** working in our accounts department for five years.*

*Managers **will have** to attend all of the regional conferences.*

*Tony **has been** taking too many sick days.*

Let's try:

We employ six regional managers, and we plan to appoint four more soon.

Sheila has worked in our accounts department for five years.

Managers must attend all of the regional conferences.

Tony takes too many sick days.

We saved six words over the four sentences. Not fantastic, I know, but useful.

Verbal Diarrhoea

Remember that misusing the passive always brings in unwanted auxiliary verbs:

The sales figures for November **have been** *analysed by the Finance Manager.*

becomes:

The Finance Manager analysed the November sales figures.

Sometimes the auxiliary verb drags in other unnecessary verbs and nouns:

The council **was** *prepared to admit that it* **had been** *negligent.*

The Education Department **will have** *to take steps to inform all parents of the arrangements for appeals.*

These could become:

The council admitted negligence.

The Education Department must inform all parents of the appeal arrangements.

Exercise: Gain from Pain

Rewrite the following, using fewer auxiliary verbs and using the present tense of the verb where possible. The original is 64 words. You can reduce it by 10 words at least, and make it seem much more direct.

A recent company report has emphasised the importance of making sure that we have trained all our sales staff properly. We have been appointing some good quality people, but even the best staff have complained that they have received little detailed information about the products they have been selling. To remedy this, the company will have to introduce new sales training procedures next month. *(64 words)*

Possible Rewrite

A recent company report emphasises the importance of making sure that we train all our sales staff properly. We appoint some good quality people, but even the best staff complain that they receive little detailed information about the products they sell. To remedy this, the company introduces new sales training procedures next month. *(53 words)*

'You are what you eat,' they say, but not according to the website for Burger King.

Burger King Corporation makes no claim that The BK Veggie Burger or any other of its products meets the requirements of a vegan or vegetarian diet.

Or 'the requirements' of clear product labelling, I presume?

WRITING MYTH 6
You Can't Have a Comma Before *And*

A strange and persistent myth, this, especially in British English. It is complete nonsense, and it is dangerous because it undermines your ability to write clearly. So forget it!

We use a comma to show a pause in phrase or meaning, and it is no problem when we do this and the next word is 'and'. Look at this sentence:

Our present system of calculating interest is manual and very time-consuming and leads to a loss of production because the staff need to put their telephones on hold while they do the calculations.

There is clearly a need for some punctuation before the second 'and' in that sentence. Say the sentence aloud and you can sense the pause (but don't say it too loud, or you might wake up some of your colleagues).You could use a full stop, and then begin the next sentence with the pronoun 'this' or 'it' instead of the second 'and'. Or you could add a comma before 'and'. Both are correct.

Yankee Doodle Comma

Where did this myth come from? I think from confusing two different types of comma: the 'listing comma' and the 'joining comma'. The listing comma actually stands for the word 'and'. It works like this:

Our lives are miserable, laborious, and short.

There's a cheerful thought for you. The comma after 'miserable' does the work of 'and'.

And here we come to a difference between UK and US usage. The average Brit (like me) would not have put the final comma in that sentence, but the average American would. The Brits do it this way:

Our lives are miserable, laborious and short.

We Brits like to think that the Yanks are ruining 'our' language. But the truth is that the more common American way is the old-fashioned style, and the British way is a modern invention. In fact, some Ancient Britons still do it the American way: it's called the 'Oxford comma', as in Oxford University. (I'm glad I went to Cambridge!)

However, in some listing sentences you *must* use the final comma to avoid ambiguity, whichever side of the Atlantic Ocean you're writing on:

The couples dancing were Ricky and Susan, Terry and Mindy, and Robert and Julie.

But the listing comma, which in nearly all cases stands for 'and', is very different from the joining comma, which can't normally stand for 'and'. And this is where the myth of 'no commas before ands' can be dangerous. This type of sentence, although now common, is not good grammar:

Michael will be attending the meeting on Tuesday, he will bring the latest sales brochure.

When you use a joining comma to join two complete sentences, you must follow the comma with a suitable joining word (generally *and, or, but, while* or *yet*).

*Michael will be attending the meeting on Tuesday, **and** he will bring the latest sales brochure.*

You'll need to remember that there are some words that you can't use after a joining comma: words such as 'however', 'therefore', 'consequently' and 'nevertheless'. Don't write:

I was supposed to go to the conference, however I was ill.

In this instance the comma should be a full stop, or a semicolon. And 'however', as the first word of a sentence, is followed by a comma:

However, it was in April of 1996 that I first visited New York.

Forgetting the comma after 'however' is a too common mistake.

To sum up: you don't always need a comma before 'and' but, when you do, put it in!

So that's another school grammar myth laid low, and not a moment too soon.

For more details on the comma, see **Grammar tip 10**.

Lawyers don't give much away, and when they do they don't like to admit it. This is from a legal contract.

The Guarantor shall not by paying any sum due hereunder or by any means or on any ground claim or recover by the institution of proceedings or the threat of proceedings or otherwise such sum from the Contractor or claim any set-off or counterclaim against the Contractor or prove in competition with the Employer in respect of any payment by the Guarantor hereunder or be entitled in competition with the Employer to claim or have the benefit of any security which the Employer holds or may hold for any money or liabilities due or incurred by the Contractor to the Employer and in case the Guarantor receives any sums from the Contractor in respect of any payment of the Guarantor hereunder the Guarantor shall hold such monies in trust for the Employer so long as any sums are payable (contingently or otherwise) under this Agreement.

Did you know that lawyers can buy special computer keyboards that don't have any punctuation keys?

GRAMMAR TIP 7
My Husband and I

Every time Her Majesty Queen Elizabeth II (long may she reign) begins a speech with 'My husband and I' she causes some grammatical confusion in the UK. Not that the Queen ever makes a grammatical mistake (off to the Tower of London with you for even suggesting it), but some of her subjects do. Many of the Queen's subjects can't get their **personal pronouns** right. And to make sure that they do, the Queen has appointed me Her Majesty's Inspector General of Pronouns (an unpaid post).

So what is a personal pronoun? A personal pronoun takes the place of a personal noun. Personal pronouns make sentences run more smoothly. For instance:

The chief executive wrote to the shareholders to tell the shareholders of the poor annual dividend.

becomes (personal pronoun in bold):

*The chief executive wrote to the shareholders to tell **them** of the poor annual dividend.*

And this sentence:

Rachel had a headache because Rachel had been working at the computer too long.

becomes:

*Rachel had a headache because **she** had been working at the computer too long.*

The personal pronouns change their form depending on whether they stand for the **subject** (generally coming before the verb) or **object** (coming after the verb, and often after a **preposition** such as *to, with, for, from*) in a sentence, or they are **possessive**, when someone owns something:

*I gave the book to **him**.*

*He gave the book to **me**.*

*We often go to France with **them**.*

*They often go to France with **us**.*

*This is **my** book, but that book is **yours**.*

*That is **your** book, but this book is **mine**.*

Most of us rarely make mistakes with personal pronouns when they are coming at us one at a time, even if we handle them instinctively rather than under-stand the grammar. But when we have to handle personal pronouns in pairs or with proper nouns, there is a worrying tendency to come up with sentences such as:

*Peter was given the report by Jane and **I** yesterday.*

This is wrong. The appearance of Jane in this sentence has led us into the trap of using *I* when we should have used *me*. If we left Jane out, we would get it right.

*Peter was given the report by **me** yesterday.*

When Jane comes into the sentence that is no reason to change *me* to *I*. But the Queen says 'My husband and I', you're thinking. Her Majesty certainly does, but she always gets it right. She says:

*My husband and **I** will be undertaking an official visit to Canada in June.*

'My husband' and 'I' are the subjects of that sentence. But she would certainly say (and she would be right):

*Canada will receive an official visit in June from my husband and **me**.*

because 'my husband' and 'me' are the objects of that sentence. So it's correct to say:

*So it's goodnight from Fiona and **me**.*

Because if you forget Fiona (and who could?) you wouldn't say:

*So it's goodnight from **I**.*

Nor would the following be correct:

*She asked Peter and **I** to write the report.*

This should be:

*She asked Peter and **me** to write the report.*

Sentences such as this are common, especially in casual speech:

*Mike and **me** [or **Me** and Mike] went to the pub last night.*

However, in writing we must be careful to get the pronouns right:

*Mike and **I** went to the pub last night.*

Leave the other person out and you will always choose the right pronoun.

Actors are good with words, aren't they? Here's Richard Gere, as quoted in a newspaper interview.

```
I know who I am. No one else knows who I
am. If I was a giraffe and somebody said
I was a snake, I'd think, 'No, actually,
I am a giraffe.'
```

From *American Gigolo* to American Gobbledygook. Give that man an Oscar.

Selfish Writers

Another common problem with personal pronouns is that writers misuse the pronouns *myself* and *yourself*. We call these **reflexive pronouns**. Use them only as emphasising words, or to refer back to the subject of the verb. Correct uses are:

*I did this **myself**.*

*He washes **himself**.*

*They must serve **themselves**.*

*Can't you dress **yourself**?*

Incorrect uses are:

The visit will be made by Ms Jones   (Use **me**.)
*and **myself**.*

*They made **myself** and my wife*   (Use **me**.)
very welcome.

*It seemed that Jimmy and **yourself***   (Use **you**.)
were being picked on.

John's sense of insecurity was plain   (Use **me**.)
*to Susan and **myself**.*

Just leave out the other person and you will get this right.

Sentences like the following, although not technically incorrect, do seem pointless:

*I **myself** am of the opinion.*

Why not simply 'I am of the opinion' or 'I think'? Far from intensifying certainty, *myself* here seems to weaken the sentence, and to suggest uncertainty.

Exercise: Gain from Pain

Change the incorrect personal pronouns in these sentences.

1. Me and my sister went to the opera last night.

2. It was important for my sister and I to go to the opera before we left Paris.

3. John and me gave instructions to the new staff.

4. The new staff told Shirley and I that they needed more training.

5. Her and Bill introduced the new procedures in April.

6. The police forced Patrick and he to take a breathalyser test.

7. Mary asked Tony and myself to stay late.

8. When yourself and Dave arrive at the hotel, please notify myself straight away.

Answers

Corrected pronouns in bold.

1. My sister and **I** went to the opera last night.

2. It was important for my sister and **me** to go to the opera before we left Paris.

3. John and **I** gave instructions to the new staff.

4. The new staff told Shirley and **me** that they needed more training.

5. **She** and Bill introduced the new procedures in April.

6. The police forced Patrick and **him** to take a breathalyser test.

7. Mary asked Tony and **me** to stay late.

8. When **you** and Dave arrive at the hotel, please notify **me** straight away.

WRITING MYTH 7

Shall We Use *Will*?

Take down that dusty old grammar book from your bookshelf. You don't have a dusty old grammar book on your bookshelf? You don't even have a bookshelf? Well, if you had, you would probably be surprised to read the section on using the verbs *will* and *shall*. Once upon a time there was a distinction in the use of these two verbs. One to do with *future time* and the other to do with *intention* or *determination* to do something.

Future Time

For future time, grammars used to demand the following pattern (using *arrive* as an example):

I/We **shall** *arrive on Thursday.*

You **will** *arrive on Thursday.*

He/She/They/It **will** *arrive on Thursday.*

In other words, it was wrong to say:

*I **will** arrive next Thursday.*

But as the *Comprehensive Grammar of the English Language* puts it (page 320, if you don't believe me), 'Prescriptive tradition forbids *will* as a future auxiliary with *I* or *we*, but this prescription is old-fashioned and is nowadays widely ignored.' Well said. We will, or we shall, or we would, or we could all agree with that, I'm sure.

Intention or Determination

For intention to do something ('volition' is the fancy word), *will* was preferred after *I* or *we*, and *shall* after *you, he, she, it, they*.

So now you know the old rules. But, truth be told, *shall* is becoming less common in modern English, as compared with *will*. We do still use *shall* to make suggestions, give orders, or ask questions:

*What **shall** we do on Saturday?*

***Shall** we have bacon for breakfast?*

*Let's have dinner tonight, **shall** we?*

And lawyers still use *shall* in legal documents when setting out regulations:

*The tenant **shall** pay the rent every four weeks.*

Here, presumably, *shall* means *must*. And, as a non-lawyer, I can't help thinking that *must* would be stronger here.

The best rule these days, once again, is follow your ear. If *will* or *shall* sounds like the usual polite form then it is certainly acceptable for you to write it.

The same applies to the past forms of *will* and *shall*: *would* and *should*. Use what sounds natural and polite. A new boss once took great pleasure in crossing out my 'I would be grateful if …' in a memo I had written, and replacing it with 'I should be grateful if …' I shouldn't be surprised if he's still doing it. I would hope he's happy in his work.

Shall we continue?

A recent survey said that seven out of ten workers would prefer a grander-sounding job title to a salary rise. The survey also revealed some of the stranger job titles that now exist. Can you guess the usual title for these jobs?

A Optical illuminator enhancer
B Regional head of services, infrastructure and procurement
C Head of verbal communications
D Ambient replenishment controller

Answers: A Window cleaner, B Caretaker, C Receptionist, D Supermarket shelf-stacker.

GRAMMAR TIP 8
Owning Up

English, as I've said before, has a relatively simple grammar. Unlike other languages, it doesn't, for instance, require us to change the endings of our words too often. Changes in word endings, technically called 'inflections', are common in other languages. But much English grammar simply consists of getting the words in the right order. This may explain why many writers have trouble when they do occasionally have to think about word endings.

In particular, many writers have trouble handling the apostrophe. The apostrophe, or 'the wandering tadpole', as I call it, causes endless problems. It's forever turning up when it's not wanted, and missing when it should be there. The bad news is that people communicating in the business world must get their apostrophes right all the time. The government may abolish apostrophes one day (I hear a big cheer). But, until then, get them right.

In this chapter we'll look at the apostrophe's role in showing possession. The technical name for this in grammar is the **genitive**. The genitive is made by adding *s* to a noun, and by putting an apostrophe before the *s*:

*the **boy's** books*

*the **dog's** home*

That's all right if there's just one boy. But what if we are talking about books belonging to more than one boy? We'd obviously add *s* to show the plural, so where do we put the apostrophe? In this case the apostrophe just hangs after the final *s*:

*the **boys'** books*

*the **dogs'** home*

Although many people despise the apostrophe and argue that English could survive well without it, we can see from these examples that it is useful. It gives us information about the number of people owning the books, or the number of dogs in the home, that we couldn't get in any other way.

But what happens when the plural of the noun doesn't end in *s*, as all good regular nouns should? What about *man*, for instance? We're obviously confident when it's just one man:

the **man's** shoes

'But surely the plural of *man* is not *mans*?' you're thinking. And you're right. So what do we do when we want to write about more than one man's shoes? We simply put the apostrophe before the final genitive *s*:

the **men's** shoes

In the same way (using nouns with regular plurals as examples):

the **electrician's** tools	(one electrician)
the **electricians'** tools	(more than one)
the **director's** briefcase	(one director)
the **directors'** briefcases	(more than one)
the **worker's** rights	(one worker)
the **workers'** rights	(the working class)

And, using nouns with irregular plurals:

the **woman's** clothes	(one woman)
the **women's** clothes	(more than one woman)
the **child's** toys	(one kid)
the **children's** toys	(too many kids)

The rules stay the same even for other, even more irregular, plurals:

*the **lady's** hats*	(one refined woman with many hats)
*the **ladies'** hats*	(more than one refined woman – probably from the **Women's** Institute)
*the **person's** rights*	(one citizen)
*the **people's** rights*	(the whole democracy)
*the **boss's** perks*	(just one chief)
*the **bosses'** perks*	(too many chiefs?)

To summarise the rules about showing possession:

- If the possessive noun is singular, we add an apostrophe and the letter *s*.

- If the possessive noun is plural and ends with *s*, as most English nouns do, then we add an apostrophe at the end of the word.

- If the plural of the noun doesn't end with *s*, then we add an apostrophe and then *s*.

Of Mice and Men

We do have another way of showing possession in English, called the **of-genitive** (in bold in these examples):

the boat's sails
*the sails **of the boat***

football's future
*the future **of football***

the children's answers
*the answers **of the children***

As you can see, the of-genitive takes more words. Now you've mastered the apostrophe, you have no excuse for using the of-genitive just because it means you don't have to worry about where to put the apostrophe!

One final point: proper nouns (the names of people or places) that end in *s* usually take an apostrophe and the genitive *s*. So:

James's *birthday*

Mr Parsons's *complaint*

Paris's *beauty*

Keats's *poetry*

Leaving out the final *s* isn't wrong, as long as you put in the apostrophe. But if we don't pronounce an extra *s* then we just put the apostrophe after the final *s*:

Socrates' *philosophy*

Ulysses' *adventures*

Hastings' *streets*

For more about the apostrophe see **Grammar tip 9**.

Exercise: Gain from Pain

You've got three tasks in these sentences: change the of-genitives into apostrophe genitives, put in any missing apostrophes, and also correct any incorrect apostrophes.

1. The opinion of Thomas was that the staffs telephone technique had to be improved.

2. The dogs home is not the most attractive of Batterseas building's.

3. Greengrocer's shops are a major source of incorrect apostrophe's.

4. This shop sell's mens shoes, childrens' books, lady's clothes and electricians tools.

5. The proposals of the committee were put before the students representative's.

Answers

1. Thomas's opinion was that the staff's telephone technique had to be improved.

2. The dogs' home is not the most attractive of Battersea's buildings.

3. Greengrocers' shops are a major source of incorrect apostrophes.

4. This shop sells men's shoes, children's books, ladies' clothes and electricians' tools.

5. The committee's proposals were put before the students' representatives.

United States Secretary of Defense Donald Rumsfeld lays it on the line.

Reports that say something hasn't happened are always interesting to me, because as we know, there are known knowns; there are things we know we know. We also know there are known unknowns; that is to say we know there are some things we do not know. But there are also unknown unknowns — the ones we don't know we don't know.

Do you think that he knows something we don't know? Do you think we'll ever know?

WRITING MYTH 8
He, She or *They*?

The English language has more words than any other, but it lacks one very useful word. English doesn't have a *common-gender, third-person-singular pronoun.* What am I talking about? Have a look at this sentence:

A good writer always checks their spelling.

Anything wrong there? There is, according to some pedantic grammarians. *Writer* is singular, but *their* is, technically, plural. Strict grammarians would insist that we rewrite this sentence 'correctly' in some way:

*Good **writers** always check **their** spelling.*

*A good **writer** always checks **his** spelling.*

*A good **writer** always checks **his** or **her** spelling.*

The first sentence does not seem as precise as our original. The second is sexist. And the third is clumsy.

I'll stick with the first one. But now, I hope, you see what I mean when I say that English has no *common-gender, third-person-singular pronoun*. Writers used to get around this by using *he*, *him* or *his* to refer to both men and women. But you don't have to be at the cutting edge of modern feminism to see that this is not generally acceptable to most women these days.

They Died with their Boots On

I feel sure, and this is a common opinion now, that within a few years everybody will accept the plural *they*, *their* and *them* as completely correct singular words as well as plural. Soon none of us, even the most pedantic of the grammar police, will object to sentences such as:

> *If a **customer** writes in to complain, we must reply to **them*** [instead of **him or her**] *within seven days.*

> *Any **student** applying for a grant must send in **their*** [instead of **his or her**] *form by 21 April 2006.*

Good writers, for the last 400 years, have broken this 'rule' of grammar. Any claim that it will lead to ambiguity is completely blown apart when we notice that English has operated for many years with only one form of *you*. The old singular forms *thee* and *thou* are now as dead as the dodo, except in a few traditional contexts. Juliet still needs her *thou* when she is talking about Romeo on that balcony.

English grammar has made things even more difficult for itself by classing as singular several words that the average person (if there is such an animal) would think of as plural:

each, either, neither, nobody, anyone, everyone, everybody

So this sentence is wrong, according to traditional rules:

Everyone *should take* **their** *time cards to the office.*

We would have to change *their* to *his or her* to agree with the 'singular' *everyone*. This 'rule' even confused Shakespeare: 'God send everyone their heart's desire.' Didn't Will realise he should have written: 'God send everyone his or her heart's desire'? If the Bard is fooled, what hope for us mere mortals? Must you really walk around the office holding that mobile you've found and shouting,

Has **anyone** *lost* **his or her** *phone?*

You would feel a bit silly saying that, wouldn't you? Language changes. We must change with it when the change seems sensible. There seems little sense in defending a 'rule' that we contradict all the time in good speech and writing.

If you really feel you can't break this 'rule', or the person you write for won't let you break it, then the sensible way forward is to rewrite the sentence so that it is not clumsy or sexist. Let's look at some examples.

*Everyone should take **their** time cards to the office.*

This could become:

*All staff should take **their** time cards to the office.*

All is a plural word, so even the strictest grammarian would allow us to use *their* in this case.
What about this sentence?

*Anybody who wants to work overtime should let **their** line manager know right away.*

If you are convinced that you are breaking a rule here, you could try using *you*:

*If **you** plan to work overtime, let **your** line manager know right away.*

And a last example:

*Everybody has the right to defend **himself** if he is attacked.*

Sexist? Well try:

Everybody has the right of self-defence if attacked.

Whatever you do, don't write nonsense such as *he/she* or *his/her* or, even worse, *(s)he*. None of these are good English. The forward slash is not a proper punctuation mark.

We all use jargon sometimes, but military jargon has a strange charm all of its own. This is from a US Marine Corps patrol report from the Vietnam War.

The patrol discovered a person in a non-viable condition.

Thank God for that, because for one terrible moment I thought the person might be dead, not simply 'non-viable'.

GRAMMAR TIP 9
More about the Wandering Tadpole

You can probably divide the population of Britain into two: 50 per cent know nothing of apostrophes, care less, and take pleasure in not using them, or putting them in whenever they feel like it. The other 50 per cent are proud of knowing how to use them correctly, and, the minute they spot an incorrect apostrophe, will not take you seriously as a writer. They'll think less of you and the organisation that employs you. As a professional, you should place yourself firmly in the second 50 per cent.

Grammar tip 8 gives you information about using the apostrophe to show possession, and **Writing myth 5** about using it when you use contractions. This chapter will tidy up the rest of the apostrophe problem.

One persistent misuse of the apostrophe is putting it before the *s* in straightforward plurals. Many shopkeepers make this mistake. I passed a stall in our local market a few months ago sporting the wonderful sign:

Barrys delicious seafood − shrimp's, eel's, whelk's, mussel's.

Four apostrophes where they are not needed, and one apostrophe missing:

Barry's delicious seafood − shrimps, eels, whelks, mussels.

If Barry hadn't been so big I would have spoken to him about this. It's a very common error. People are always trying to persuade me that they sell *TV's, video's, computer's* and so on. They don't: they sell *TVs, videos, computers.* I don't want to buy the unwanted apostrophe as well. A restaurant I was in a short time ago told me that they sold *pizza's* on the menu. I knocked back two bottles of wine with the meal to wash away the memory of that apostrophe. But it still haunts me.

The *TV's* mistake is the most common. Just because this is an abbreviation as well as a plural there's still no need to put in an apostrophe. The other case where writers often make this mistake is with dates: the *1990's* and so on. The *1990s* is the best form these days. And don't use the apostrophe when you are pluralising the name of someone or something. This is wrong:

There are three Mike's in my office, and they all drive BMW's.

Leave the apostrophes out: *Mikes* and *BMWs* are correct here. You keep up with the *Joneses*, not the *Jones's*.

We do use the apostrophe when we (rarely) need to pluralise a letter of the alphabet. This prevents confusion. Thus:

> *Do you know how many s's there are in Massachusetts?*

> *Don't forget to dot your i's and to cross your t's, and mind your p's and q's.*

> *You mustn't confuse your e.g.'s and your i.e.'s, and never use too many etc.'s.*

The Time is Right

We still use the apostrophe to measure out periods of time. Most writers get this right if they are writing about one day, week, month or year:

> *I've taken only one day's annual leave so far.*

> *We're taking one week's holiday in France.*

> *He owes the landlord one month's rent.*

> *I have one year's experience of personnel management.*

It may seem strange that we use an apostrophe in these sentences, but the apostrophe here is really standing for *of*: one month *of* holiday, one day *of* annual leave. When there is more than one day, week, month or year we must still get the apostrophe right. Nothing unusual happens here: you simply put the apostrophe after the plural *s*. So, using the four sentences above:

I've taken only three days' annual leave so far.

We're taking two weeks' holiday in France.

He owes the landlord two months' rent.

I have five years' experience of personnel management.

We don't use the apostrophe when we use a possessive pronoun: *yours*, *theirs*, *its* and so on. And remember: *it's* is a shortened form of *it is*. *Its* means 'belongs to it'. Try the sentence with *it is* if you're ever thinking of using *it's* . You'll soon see when you've made a mistake:

The horse has broken it's leg.

should be:

The horse has broken its leg.

Do that again, and the grammar police will break your leg.

Exercise: Gain from Pain

Correct the apostrophe mistakes in these sentences. You will need to use all the information you have learned about apostrophes, not just in this chapter but also in Grammar tip 8 and Writing myth 5. So read those chapters again before you start.

1. When my cat licks it's paws then Im sure its hungry.

2. James holiday was one weeks walking in the mountain's of Spain.

3. There playing on the football field's even though its raining cat's and dogs.

4. When Thomas get's back from school your both going to the barbers.

5. Mr Smith owe's the citys housing authority three months rent, and hell be evicted if it isnt paid soon.

6. Whose thought these sentences up? There giving me a headache – and thats the truth!

Answers

1. When my cat licks its paws then I'm sure it's hungry.

2. James's holiday was one week's walking in the mountains of Spain.

3. They're playing on the football fields even though it's raining cats and dogs.

4. When Thomas gets back from school you're both going to the barber's.

5. Mr Smith owes the city's housing authority three months' rent, and he'll be evicted if it isn't paid soon.

6. Who's thought these sentences up? They're giving me a headache – and that's the truth!

Many cynics say that you have to go to university before you really learn how not to write. They may be right. This is from the GENIUS (I kid you not!) Project of the University of Reading.

The project is structured around multi-faceted incremental work plan combining novel content design based on new pedagogical paradigms blended with the e-learning environments to facilitate hybrid mode of delivery. This is combined with series of educational experiments on the target learner groups with possibilities to adjust the approach and disseminate the interim and final results. Our pedagogical approach is based on the educational model which assumes that the learning process is an interactive process of seeking understanding, consisting of three fundamental components: Conceptualisation, Construction and Dialogue. The relevant modules of the New Curricula are mapped onto these three components and a hybrid way of delivery is investigated through different scenarios.

So go to Reading for some poor reading.

WRITING MYTH 9
That and *Which* Are Interchangeable

Look at these two sentences. What's the difference between them?

Snakes that are poisonous should be avoided.

Snakes, which are poisonous, should be avoided.

That's right, the second sentence is telling you that *all* snakes are poisonous. Whereas the first is telling you (correctly, I think) that only some snakes are poisonous. Personally, I'd avoid all snakes, but that has nothing to do with grammar, just fear.

The first sentence has what we call a **restrictive** (or **defining**) **clause**, restricting the snakes we should avoid to poisonous ones only. The second has a **nonrestrictive** (or **nondefining**) **clause**. We could have used 'which' instead of 'that' in the first sentence. But we can use only 'which' in the second. It's usually the commas that tell you that you've got to use 'which'. This sentence would be incorrect:

The report, that has taken me five weeks to write, will be published in June.

You need a 'which' there. So you can't always swap 'that' and 'which'.

You can use either 'that' or 'which' in the following two sentences:

The book that my father gave me is on the table.

The book which my father gave me is on the table.

You can even leave either of them out and write:

The book my father gave me is on the table.

When you do have a choice between 'that' and 'which', it's probably best, in most cases, to go for 'that', which is generally more natural. You should also use 'that' when 'which' occurs earlier in the sentence:

Which is the book that you bought?

And 'that' sounds better after words such as 'everything', 'anything', 'nothing' and 'something' (the indefinite pronouns). So write:

There is everything here that you need.

Who's Who?

Despite what some people tell you, you can use 'that' to replace 'who' or 'whom' in some sentences. This sentence is acceptable:

The woman that I saw was wearing a red dress.

Even neater would be:

The woman I saw was wearing a red dress.

But we do use 'which' after a preposition:

Is this the photograph to which you were referring?

If we do use 'that' in such a sentence, then the preposition must go to the end:

Is this the photograph that you were referring to?

Or even:

Is this the photograph you were referring to?

Congratulations: you've learned a bit of 'which–craft' now.

Some people are frightened of flying. Personally, I'm more frightened of British Airways' prose style. This is from their terms and conditions. Prepare for some verbal turbulence.

CHARGES FOR CHANGES AND CANCELLATIONS

NOTE-CANCELLATIONS-BEFORE DEPARTURE FARE IS REFUNDABLE. IF COMBINING A NON-REFUNDABLE FARE WITH A REFUNDABLE FARE ONLY THE Y/C/J-CLASS HALF RETURN AMOUNT CAN BE REFUNDED. AFTER DEPARTURE FARE IS REFUNDABLE. IF COMBINING A NON-REFUNDABLE FARE WITH A REFUNDABLE FARE REFUND THE DIFFERENCE/IF ANY/BETWEEN THE FARE PAID AND APPLICABLE NORMAL BA ONEWAY FARE.

Now read that again. But this time, fasten your safety belt.

GRAMMAR TIP 10

Putting Commas in Their Place

People often say that a comma shows a pause in a sentence. There is some truth to this, but it's sometimes misleading. As I said earlier, saying a sentence aloud often shows you the pause. But many commas can come down to a matter of style: you may hear a more definite pause than I do. Look at the following sentences:

If the Seaview Hotel is booked, we can always try another one.

By the time I arrived, the party was almost over.

Both the commas in these sentences are technically correct, and they do give a certain structure to the sentences. We would still understand them if we left the commas out, but a good stylist generally puts them in.

It is traditional to put a comma after an **adverb** at the beginning of a sentence:

Unfortunately, Cathy has come down with the flu.

Frankly, I don't like her much.

Generally, senior staff from all departments attend the management seminar.

But in the next sentences the commas, although possible, may seem too heavy:

Yet again, we find ourselves at the bottom of the performance table.

In the summer of 1914, few people realised that a terrible war was soon to begin.

But many commas are not optional. They are essential to bring out the sense of a sentence. Leaving them out, or misplacing them, causes confusion or even changes your meaning.

For instance, we must use a comma to break off an introduction to a sentence if the reader might misread the sentence without the comma:

Once senior management decides staff have to follow that decision whether they agree with it or not.

After the judge concludes it is the task of the jury to consider their verdict.

Both these sentences need a comma to bring out their true meaning clearly:

Once senior management decides, staff have to follow that decision whether they agree with it or not.

After the judge concludes, it is the task of the jury to consider their verdict.

We also use a comma to mark off a long introductory idea in a sentence. Look at these examples:

Although the hospital management does not currently intend to do so on a regular basis, it may recruit 25 per cent more agency nurses over the next three months to deal with the number of emergency admissions caused by the present flu epidemic.

Because there are too many games and because of the injuries caused to players by fatigue, the league is considering reducing the number of teams.

According to a report issued this morning by the Press Association, the president of Dunroamia was assassinated by two hooded gunmen last night while leaving the theatre.

These sentences would be far more difficult to read and understand without the commas.

Don't Get Spliced

You should not usually join two sentences with a comma without putting a joining word after the comma. This is usually called the 'comma splice'.

I gave the report to Jim on Tuesday, he didn't read it until Wednesday.

She married him in October, he hasn't been the same man since.

These commas could become full stops or (perish the thought) semicolons. But as commas they must be followed with a suitable conjunction:

I gave the report to Jim on Tuesday, but he didn't read it until Wednesday.

She married him in October, and he hasn't been the same man since.

Poor writers misuse one type of comma more than any other: what we call **bracketing commas**. Note that I've used the plural *commas*. Bracketing commas come in pairs (like brackets). Missing out one of the commas, or even both of them, is too common among careless writers.

We use a bracketing comma *each side* of additional information in a sentence. Here are some examples. Note that we could leave out the words between the bracketing commas (as they form a nonrestrictive clause) but still have a complete sentence:

The Cancer Research Campaign's study, published last May, gives detailed figures for rates of prostate cancer.

Admissions tutors, who rely on predicted rather than actual grades, deny being biased against applicants from state schools.

A solution, obvious for some time, is private pensions built up while in employment.

(See **Writing myth 9** for more on nonrestrictive clauses.)

And sometimes putting in bracketing commas can change the meaning of the sentence:

Managers who are incompetent will be dismissed.

Managers, who are incompetent, will be dismissed.

Putting the bracketing commas in the second sentence makes it seem that all your managers are incompetent. And I'm sure that's not true!

Don't Dash Off

You can use a pair of dashes (–) in place of bracketing commas for a bit of variety. But don't overuse the dash (often called the 'en dash' or 'en rule' on a computer). Too many of them make it look as if you haven't quite finished editing your writing. They can look a bit slapdash, in other words. Keep the dash for special occasions. I use the dash only for a bit of drama at the end of a sentence:

And we all know who was responsible for this mess – Terry Denman!

For a dismissal of the nonsensical myth that you can't have a comma before *and*, see **Writing myth 6**.

Exercise: Gain from Pain

Put the commas in these sentences.

1. Unfortunately Tony's report although detailed was not completely accurate.

2. Published in 1948 when he was only twenty-one Maurice Dobb's first novel was rapturously received by the critics and sold millions.

3. He was born in Wimbledon a suburb of southwest London.

4. If we lose any more staff which looks likely we will be in a desperate position and possibly forced to close down some if not all of our operations.

5. When Jane finally arrived just before midnight I could see that she was contented although tired and hungry.

Possible Rewrites

The optional commas are within brackets.

1. Unfortunately, Tony's report, although detailed, was not completely accurate.

2. Published in 1948, when he was only twenty-one, Maurice Dobb's first novel was rapturously received by the critics(,) and sold millions.

3. He was born in Wimbledon, a suburb of southwest London.

4. If we lose any more staff, which looks likely, we will be in a desperate position(,) and possibly forced to close down some; if not all, of our operations.

5. When Jane finally arrived, just before midnight, I could see that she was contented, although tired and hungry.

Where would we be without the benefit of modern communications? This is from Trilogy Telecom's email to a customer.

BT have started processing the first stage of our MPF orders i.e. the line test and production of a line characteristics report. However with the second stage (i.e. physically installing the metallic facility path between the customers line and the Trilogy equipment) they will only walk one or two orders through the system Thursday of next week.

I hope that while they are 'physically installing the metallic facility path' they remember to 'lay the cable' as well.

WRITING MYTH 10

You Mustn't Use the Same Word Too Often

A terrible disease is stalking our green and pleasant land. The disease is *synonymitis*. Doctors disagree about the origin of the disease, but think it's probably caused by too much exposure to thesauruses (or thesauri – both are acceptable). The thesaurus gives you synonyms: words that mean the same, or roughly the same, as the word you are looking up.

The thesaurus is a wonderful book. I own one, but use it with caution. The literal meaning of *thesaurus* (from the Ancient Greek, as I'm sure you knew) is 'treasure store'. A thesaurus is full of treasures: the treasures of the English language. But, as with all treasures, spend it wisely. In other words, don't use a £5 word when a 5p one will do. In fact, use the thesaurus to find the best, and the simplest, word that will do the job effectively. And, when you've found that word, stick with it.

But many writers can't do this. They start a letter or report quite sensibly with an effective, simple word such as *begin*. After a few *begin*s they start imagining that the reader will be getting bored or annoyed. So they pick up the office thesaurus. Next to *begin* they spot *commence*, and start using that for a paragraph or two. Now they think we're getting bored with *commence*, and out comes that thesaurus again. This time they spot *initiate*. And after half a dozen of those they go back to *begin* again. Yes, they've caught synonymitis. Quick, nurse, draw the curtains. Or, if you suffer from synonymitis:

Be expeditious, medical ancillary, and envelop the patient's sleeping chamber with the privacy screens.

A thesaurus is there for you to find the *right* word for the task. Once you've found that word it will almost certainly be the right word throughout the document. Changing it for no other reason than 'a bit of variety' will damage your writing, not improve it.

Pretentious, *moi*?

Teachers give you extra marks for using different words all the time. They are, laudably, trying to build up your vocabulary. But, in the real world, taking your readers for a little trip through the thesaurus is not good style.

In the first place, you will keep changing the tone of your document. The thesaurus gives you lots of different words, but the words range in tone from the friendly and everyday, to the prissy and pompous, up to the downright haughty. Any sensible reader will find the changes of tone as you scuttle through the thesaurus puzzling.

Second, not all your readers (especially if you're writing for a wide audience) will understand words from the furthest edges of the thesaurus. Most people will probably (we hope!) understand *begin* and *commence*. But *initiate*, *instigate* or *inaugurate*, or whatever unlikely word you come up with next, may well cause problems. In other words, your overuse of the thesaurus may force the reader to use a dictionary.

Third, few so-called synonyms actually match exactly. Your writing will be less precise if you consult the thesaurus too often. Sometimes to amusing effect. I was once editing a company report about the procedures that staff had to follow when moving goods out of warehouses. Naturally, the word 'warehouse' cropped up quite often. Unfortunately, the writer of the report began to worry about this after a few paragraphs. All of a sudden I was reading about a 'static storage facility'. Now a warehouse is normally static, and it is for storage. But a 'static storage facility' isn't necessarily a warehouse. We could describe a fixed cupboard as a 'static storage facility'. Warehouses are happy as warehouses, and cupboards as cupboards. It's best to leave them that way. Don't give them ideas above their station in life.

No one is trying to deprive you of your right to use any word you like, so long as you are convinced it is the best word available. But the idea that you are overusing a word is, in most cases, more of a problem for the writer than the reader.

Don't feel that you have to use a word so that it doesn't die of neglect. If a word has a useful role in English, it will survive. If it doesn't, it will die. And remember your patriotic duty: if you notice a word dying, go over and kick it, don't give it the kiss of life. We all have to go to the great dictionary in the sky when the time comes.

Going for fancy words from the thesaurus often means that writers end up with egg on their faces. A report I edited a few months back told me that 'Mr Smith had been *appraised* of the situation in June 2003.' The writer meant 'apprised'. But 'informed', 'told' and 'notified' would all have been more sensible options.

If you really feel that you're using a word too often in a short space and you *must* change, then make a sensible change. What is the next commonest word? The thesaurus on a word processor or computer usually gives some weird and wonderful synonyms. I've just tried *student* on mine. It came up with:

pupil   (Wouldn't be the correct term for a
             university student, say.)

scholar   (If only all students were scholars.)

disciple   (Theology students only, I presume.)

apprentice (Few of those about these days.)

observer   (Isn't a student supposed to do a bit more
             than observe?)

docent   (Even I had to look that one up!)

Lots of fun, these thesauruses (or thesauri). But not always helpful.

You've probably tossed and turned at night wondering how to define a container. Here comes the Department of Health to your rescue. This is from the *Medicines for Human Use (Clinical Trials) Regulations* of 2004.

'Container', in relation to an investigational medicinal product, means the bottle, jar, box, packet or other receptacle which contains or is to contain it, not being a capsule, cachet or other article in which the product is or is to be administered, and where any such receptacle is or is to be contained in another such receptacle, includes the former but does not include the latter receptacle.

That sentence contains a lot of words, but they don't contain much sense.

APPENDIX 1

Everyday and Workaday Words

Words, words, words – English is full of them. We have more words than any other language. In fact, picking up an English dictionary is a well-known form of exercise in many foreign countries. We often use complex words to sound impressive (and show off to our colleagues!), but readers may suspect that we are using them to conceal weak ideas. And you won't be detracting from your professional image (another great fear) if you use everyday words wherever you can. The sensible reader will judge you on what you say, not the fancy way you say it. Generally, the more complicated and important the information you are trying to get across, the simpler your language should be. And fancy 'management jargon' that is all the fashion today ('parameter', 'synergy', 'proactive' and so on) soon dates. But good old plain English words never let you down!

You should always try the simplest word first. If that word won't work, then you have the treasures of the English language to draw on. Despite my rude comments, no one is saying that you can't, occasionally, use one of the words on the left. But in the workaday world you should favour the everyday words on the right. They're generally shorter, livelier and more natural. They're the words you think in, so write in them. Here are just a few of Scotland Yard's most wanted.

USE SPARINGLY   **PREFER**

additional   **more, extra**
Unless, of course, you need additional syllables because you ordered too much toner for the office printer.

apprise   **inform, tell, let you know**
Now that I've apprised you of the synonyms, use them.

ascertain   **learn, find out**
'Pass me the TV listings. I want to ascertain what's on the TV tonight.' Leave that one for the Queen.

assist   **help**
I hope that suggestion assists you.

commence   **begin, start**
Only artillery barrages commence. So, unless you're writing for the army, start to use 'begin'.

USE SPARINGLY	PREFER

component   **part**

Of course, you could write 'component part'. Then I'd be angrier than a rattlesnake with a migraine.

concept   **idea**

I thought I had a concept once, but it turned out to be a good old idea.

determine   **decide**

Be determined to use 'decide' more.

discontinue   **stop, end**

Discontinue has just been discontinued, because of lack of public interest.

due to the fact that   **as, because**

Because is better, due to the fact that it's shorter.

endeavour   **try**

When a company says it will 'endeavour' to send your money in the next few days, prepare yourself for failure!

establish   **set up, form, create**

Let's establish an 'establish-free zone'.

expedite   **hasten, speed up**

'We will endeavour to expedite your cheque.' See under *endeavour*.

facilitate   **help, make possible**

'Facilitate' is an overused word. Let's facilitate it out of its misery.

forward (*verb*)   **send, give**

Leave the forward on the football field.

implement   **carry out, do**

The implementation of 'implement' in business writing is too common.

in conjunction with   **with**

Using 'in conjunction with' too often, often goes in conjunction with gobbledygook.

initiate   **begin, start**

See under *commence*.

in lieu of   **instead of, in place of**

That's right, in lieu of 'in lieu of', use something in place of it.

in order to   **to**

In order to save toner, stop using 'in order to'.

interim   **meantime, for the time being**

Use the words on the right for the interim.

obtain   **get, receive**

Obtain a life!

USE SPARINGLY	PREFER

particulars details, facts, information

Someone once told me that they needed to 'take down' my 'particulars'. How cheeky can you get? We'd only just met.

persons people

Calling people persons makes it sound as if they're in police custody.

purchase buy

You can buy two 'buys' for one purchase.

regarding about

Regard the shorter word on the right.

remittance payment

Unless, of course, it's a very big payment.

reside live

You reside in a cemetery. You live at home.

terminate end, stop

The Terminator has ended up as governor of California. Where will he stop?

utilise use

And remember, if you leave 'utilise' for a few days and water it regularly it will grow into – 'the utilisation of'!

APPENDIX 2

Ten Ways Grammar Can Help You Fight Gobbledygook and Waffle

Good writers don't waste words. Use your grammatical knowledge to cut out the gobbledygook and waffle. Here's a 10-point summary of the preceding chapters.

1. Don't use the passive when the active works better.
The report was sent to the Finance Director by the Audit Office on 1 March 1999.
The Audit Office sent the report to the Finance Director on 1 March 1999.

2. Don't use a noun when it hides a verb.
We made the decision to raise interest rates.
We decided to raise interest rates.

3. Don't use any noun you don't need.

This affects the productivity situation in our Norwich factory.

This affects productivity in our Norwich factory.

4. Don't use a complex preposition when a simple preposition will do.

In the event of the fire alarm sounding, immediately leave the building.

If the fire alarm sounds, immediately leave the building.

5. Don't waste words at the beginning of a sentence.

It will be noted that the report emphasises thorough auditing.

The report emphasises thorough auditing.

6. Don't intensify a word unless you have to.

It is very important to write succinctly.

It is important to write succinctly.

7. Don't use an unnecessary adjective.

My past experience in personnel management has been valuable.

My experience in personnel management has been valuable.

8. Don't use unnecessary auxiliary verbs.

Toyota has been using only 177 suppliers per plant.

Toyota uses only 177 suppliers per plant.

9. Don't forget to use the imperative mood of the verb.

The order should be sent straightaway.

Send the order straightaway.

10. Don't use the of-genitive too often.

The answers of the candidates were poor.

The candidates' answers were poor.

APPENDIX 3

Glossary: The Basic Grammar Terms Explained

This is not a complete list of grammatical terms. It covers only those terms I've used in this book.

abstract noun A word that describes an idea that you can't see or touch, because it is a mental state or activity.

*You need **concentration**.*

*I value our **friendship**.*

*What **bravery** she showed!*

*Make an **analysis** of the figures.*

active voice When the 'doer' or agent comes before the verb. In the passive voice the agent comes after the verb or is missing altogether.

The dog ran after the stick. (Passive: *The stick was run after by the dog.*)

The boy kicks the ball. (Passive: *The ball is being kicked by the boy.*)
The plumber mends the leak. (Passive: *The leak is being mended by the plumber.*)
The cat sits on the mat. (Passive: *The mat is being sat on by the cat.*)

adjective A word that describes a noun. Adjectives describe a noun's shape, colour, size, characteristic or quality. They can come before or after the noun they describe.

*a **tall** man*
*the bird is **green***
*the **thoughtful** woman*
*the engine was **powerful***

adverb A word that tells you when, where or, most commonly, how a verb happens. Many adverbs end in *–ly*. But other common adverbs don't (for example, *fast, well, often, now, there, later*).

*He ran **quickly**.*
*She talked **quietly**.*
*They arrived **here**.*
*You drive **fast**.*

agent The person 'doing' the verb. If the agent is before the verb we have the active. If the agent is after the verb, or missing altogether, we have the passive.

*The **professor** gave the lecture on Thursday.*
*The lecture was given on Thursday (by the **professor**).*

articles There are two articles in grammar: the **definite article** ('the') and the **indefinite article** ('a', 'an').

auxiliary verb A verb that comes before and helps the main verb. The auxiliary verbs are *be, have, do, can, could, may, might, will, would, shall, should, must.*
*He **might** go.*
*She **has been** drinking.*
*You **must** return the form.*
*They **should** arrive soon.*
*They **do** enjoy football.*

bracketing commas Two commas that mark off a weak interruption in a sentence. We could leave out the words between the bracketing commas (as they form a non-restrictive clause) and still leave words that made sense. You can use a pair of dashes instead of bracketing commas.
The book, published in 1962, was a great success.
He had agreed, although he was a very busy man, to give the lecture.
Mr Clark – a local government officer from Luton – was arrested last night.

complex sentence A sentence with two or more ideas, and where one of the ideas depends on, or is subordinate to, the main idea. We often introduce the dependent idea with a conjunction such as *because, when, although* or *since*.
I went to the door when the doorbell rang.
I invited Mary because she is a friend of my wife.

compound sentence A sentence made up of two or more ideas. Each idea in a compound sentence could, in principle, stand as a sentence on its own. We usually link the ideas with the conjunctions *and*, *but* or *or*.

I like his new car, but I don't like his new hat.

He went to Colchester last week and he will visit Norwich this week.

conjunction A word that joins a word to a word, an idea to an idea or a sentence to a sentence.

*Cats **and** dogs make good pets.*

*He spoke to me **because** he knew I needed help.*

***But** I still got it wrong.*

contraction Two words brought together as one, with some letters left out. An apostrophe shows where the missing letters come.

I'm	*I am*
It's	*It is,* or *it has*
Let's	*Let us*

genitive The ending to a noun that shows it is owning something. We use the apostrophe to show ownership.

*the **girl's** dress*

*a **winter's** day*

*five **days'** holiday*

*the **students'** results*

imperative mood The mood of the verb that gives commands. The verb comes at the beginning of the clause, and is in its simplest form.

Sit at the back of the class.

Buy this book (please).

Take two tablets every six hours.

infinitive The base form of a verb. Usually, but not always, it has *to* before it.

to sleep

to run

to pay

intensifier A word that intensifies, or heightens, a noun or adjective. Both adverbs and adjectives can act as intensifiers.

*This is **utter** folly.* (adjective intensifier)

*It was **total** irresponsibility.* (adjective intensifier)

*I **greatly** admire his music.* (adverb intensifier)

*I **really** appreciate your offer.* (adverb intensifier)

mood Verbs come in three moods:

indicative (facts): *I **pay** the rent.*

subjunctive (possibilities): *If he should **pay** the rent.*

imperative (orders): ***Pay** the rent.*

nominalisation Turning a verb into a noun or an adjective.

*We conducted an **analysis**.* (A noun from a verb: *we analysed*)

*They reached an **agreement**.* (A noun from a verb: *we agreed*)

*The figures are **indicative** of success.* (An adjective from a verb: *the figures indicate*)

*The results are **applicable** here.* (An adjective from a verb: *the results apply*)

noun A word that denotes an object, person, place or organisation. Nouns can be **common nouns**:

dog, table, writer

or **proper nouns** (which have a capital letter):

Birmingham, Elvis, Plain English Campaign

There are also **abstract nouns**.

object The part of a sentence that shows who or what is directly affected by the verb.

*I planted **a flower**.*

*All the women have bought **new dresses**.*

of-genitive A way of showing possession that does not use the apostrophe, but puts the word *of* before the possessing noun.

the name of the ship (instead of: *the ship's name*)

the future of Japan (instead of: *Japan's future*)

the release of the prisoner (instead of: *the prisoner's release*)

passive When the 'doer' or **agent** comes after the verb or is missing altogether. In the **active** the agent comes before the verb.

The stick was run after by the dog. (Active: *The dog ran after the stick.*)

The ball is being kicked by the boy. (Active: *The boy kicks the ball.*)

The leak had been fixed by the plumber. (Active: *The plumber has fixed the leak.*)

The mat is being sat on by the cat. (Active: *The cat sits on the mat.*)

past participle The part of the verb that we use after an auxiliary, or helping, verb, and which describes a past action. Many past participles end in *−ed or −en.*

*I had **loved** her for a long time.*

*We were **driven** to school.*

*They had **sought** the thief.*

personal pronoun A word that stands in for a person. The form of the personal pronoun changes depending on whether the pronoun is the subject of the sentence, the object of the sentence or possessive.

*__I__ gave the book to **him**.*

*__He__ gave the book to **me**.*

*__My__ book is on **his** table.*

*__Her__ book is on **their** table.*

phrasal verb A verb that has a preposition or adverb attached to its main part: *to drive off, to hold down, to set up, to take over.*

preposition A word that connects two parts of a sentence to show how the parts are related in space or time. Generally, a preposition comes before a noun or pronoun. Common prepositions are *at, for, up, with, by, from, near, to, in, on.*

*I took Sheila **to** the hospital.*

*I feel very sorry **for** him.*

*I went **to** the meeting **in** Leeds.*

*Put the report **on** the desk.*

pronoun A word that stands in for a person or thing.

*Jim was ill on Tuesday, after **he** had drunk too much on Monday night.*

*The cat licks **its** paws.*

***They** gave the book to **me**.*

reflexive pronoun Pronouns that end in −*self* or −*selves.*

*John washed **himself**.*

*They shaved **themselves**.*

restrictive An idea that defines, identifies, qualifies or explains a noun, as distinct from a **nonrestrictive** idea. A nonrestrictive idea is usually within bracketing commas.

Staff who are incompetent will be dismissed.

(Restrictive: says only incompetent staff will be dismissed.)

Staff, who are incompetent, will be dismissed.

(Nonrestrictive: says all staff are incompetent.)

simple sentence A sentence with one idea is a simple sentence.

I kicked the ball.

A sentence with more than one idea will be either a
compound or a **complex sentence**.

subject The subject identifies the theme or topic of a clause
or sentence. In most cases the subject comes before the
verb.

The attendant closed the door.

Rain fell all day.

She sees her father every Sunday.

Beer, whisky and vodka are all alcoholic drinks.

tense That part of the verb that shows time: past, present or
future. Sometimes we show tense by changing the end of
the verb, and sometimes by using an auxiliary verb.

I love

I loved

I had loved

I have loved

I will love

verb A verb shows doing, having or being.

*She **reads** a lot.*

*She **has** a grammar book.*

*She **is** interested in grammar.*

FURTHER READING

There are thousands of books on grammar, punctuation and effective writing. I can't say that I've read them all, but of those I've read these four particularly impressed me.

Reference

Sylvia Chalker *The Little Oxford Dictionary of English Grammar* (Oxford University Press, 1998)
A 'little' book perhaps, but packed with information on grammar, language and punctuation. Its A-to-Z format makes it easy to use. It should provide quite enough detail for those of you with a normal social life.

Grammar

David Crystal *Rediscover Grammar* (Longman, 1998)
This book is a comprehensive, modern and lively survey of English grammar. It is also attractively designed. And the author has the perfect surname for a clear writer.

Punctuation

R.L. Trask *Penguin Guide to Punctuation* (Penguin, 1997)
This book, although short, covers all the punctuation marks in impressive detail. It gives plenty of examples of good and bad punctuation to drive the points home.

Writing

Harold Evans *Essential English for Journalists, Editors and Writers* (Pimlico, 2000)
Harold Evans ('the journalists' journalist') wrote this as a style guide for newspapers, but the early chapters in particular are a wonderful guide to good writing for all of us. The best writers are nearly always journalists, not academics, so follow the former.

Training in Writing

Perhaps the most famous organisation that trains in effective business writing is the Plain English Campaign, set up in 1979. It has worked with thousands of organisations. It also publishes some useful books. You can contact the Plain English Campaign at PO Box 3, New Mills, High Peak, SK22 4QP, United Kingdom; phone: 01663 744409; email: info@plainenglish.co.uk; website: www.plainenglish.co.uk

INDEX